Stan Bailey
5/3/83

HOW TO MANAGE
A TURNAROUND

HOW TO MANAGE
A TURNAROUND

A Senior Manager's Blueprint for Turning
an Ailing Business into a Winner

STANLEY J. GOODMAN

THE FREE PRESS
A Division of Macmillan Publishing Co., Inc.
NEW YORK

Collier Macmillan Publishers
LONDON

THE FREE PRESS
A Division of Macmillan Publishing Co., Inc.
866 Third Avenue, New York, N. Y. 10022

Collier Macmillan Canada, Inc.

Library of Congress Catalog Card Number: 82-70077

Printed in the United States of America

printing number

1 2 3 4 5 6 7 8 9 10

Library of Congress Cataloging in Publication Data

Goodman, Stanley J. (Stanley Joshua)
How to manage a turnaround.

Includes index.
1. Industrial management. I. Title.
HD31.G59 1982   658   82-70077
ISBN 0-02-912480-8   AACR2

To my wife,
producer of
priceless mini-turnarounds

Contents

of Planning. Use Your Competitors. Correctible
Errors. Success as an Enemy. Goodman's Law.
Managing Change. Authority versus Initiative.
Delegate but Don't Abdicate. How versus What.
Activity versus Achievement. Participative
Management. Scale of 10.

PART III   BUILDING THE TEAM
(THE VEHICLE)

picture; Tailored to people; Fight empire building;
Divide and multiply; Clarity; Job descriptions;
Spread too thin; Value of manpower planning.

Compensation tied to MBO; Training seminars.
Components of MBO: *Job description; Standards
of performance; Writing objectives and action
programs.*

*Watchdog of cash flow; Supervises financial
reporting; Monitors performance.*

Introduction

*I do not believe you can do today's job with
yesterday's methods and be in business
tomorrow.*

—Nelson Jackson

Turnaround is a fairly new word in the language. Words
come into being to fill a need, this one to give a vivid picture of
a situation being changed, through determined effort, from
bad to good, from going down to going up, from sickness to
health, from "Oh, my God!" to "Gee whiz!"

The desire to make a turnaround is a basic human urge,
the urge to triumph over obstacles, the self-same intelligence-
driven craving that moved *homo sapiens* from primate to primacy on this planet.

Yet in the world of business many dream about turnarounds, not enough achieve them. Notable turnarounds
make spirited reading in the business press, with full honors to
the winners. But for you who may have a turnaround gleam in

your eye and are wondering how to go about it, there has been no overall guide in print for the accomplishment of a turnaround.

This book, a distillation of many years' experience in managing and advising turnaround companies, is designed to fill this widespread need. It aims to give you the basic building blocks for your turnaround in enough detail to guide successful action, step by step. Its approach to this complex subject is practical, not academic.

While no two turnarounds are exactly alike, the fundamentals in this book apply to any turnaround. Of course, the relative amount of work needed on the various building blocks will depend on the circumstances of each case.

Moreover, while this is a book about business, its prescriptions can be successfully applied to any group activity that needs to do better. Universities, hospitals, symphonies, and government are all trying to get results through people. Their achievement of objectives can be helped by the kind of action skills presented here.

In these times, at long last, women are a rising force in business, and I agree with Edward Steichen that they are "the greatest underdeveloped resource in the world today." But in the interests of readability I respectfully ask the female reader to bear with my avoidance of those awkward locutions "he or she," "s/he," "chairperson," and the like, and since "mankind" means all humankind, to assume that in this book "man" and "he" refer to both sexes. I take as my precedent the venerable Tibetan lama who, confronted with his first American visitor, addressed him as: "Dear sir or madam as the case may be."

I express lasting thanks to my many colleagues and clients, who, in countless collaborations over the years, have been the wellsprings of what is in this book. For sources of treasured lessons learned over the years, I think of these with profound gratitude: my father, for belief in potential; Edgar A. Hahn, for standards of excellence; Georges F. Doriot, for entrepreneurial insights; Malcolm P. McNair, for conceptual accuracy; Reagan P. Connally, for imaginative goals; Leonard Strauss, for personal example; Morton D. May, for human qualities; David E. Babcock, for the pursuit of professionalism; and my wife, Alice Hahn Goodman, for confidence, taste and wisdom. In addition, my deep appreciation goes to my able assistant in this and so many other undertakings, Florence R. Klug.

HOW TO MANAGE
A TURNAROUND

PART I

Who, Me?

We are confronted with insurmountable opportunities.

—Pogo

1

The Ignored
Turnaround

We have met the enemy and he is us.

—Pogo

A distressing and dangerous phenomenon in the business world is the unrecognized turnaround situation.

THE TURNAROUND IS IN THE CLOSET

Nowadays a discerning eye scanning the American business scene can detect the need for a turnaround in company after company, industry after industry. But when we get within earshot of the management of such a company, do we hear about a turnaround? Very seldom. Unhappiness, yes, guilt feelings, maybe, but facing up to and articulating a turnaround need, hardly. The business press eagerly recounts the dramas of corporate turnarounds, and chief executive officers can see the other fellow's need for a turnaround quite clearly, but as for their own business it is a case of "Who, me?"

THE TURNAROUND-SHY MANAGER

Today's manager shies away from turnaround thinking in his own situation for reasons that a psychologist might find interesting. To speak of a turnaround for his company, he feels, is an admission of failure, a reflection on the management, and an implied commitment to do something out of the ordinary which he is not ready to face. So he tells himself that all companies have problems and his company's difficulties are currently typical of the industry. And in his letter to the stockholders in the annual report he will enumerate the factors in the economy that are to be blamed for the company's current performance, and the expected economic upturn next year that will bring better results for the company.

In fact, perish the thought, our turnaround-shy manager might not want to be seen buying this book, for that could be an admission that he is going to come to grips with a turnaround. Perhaps the book ought to come in a plain wrapper.

WHAT IS MEANT BY A TURNAROUND

The word *turnaround* has been gaining currency in the language of business but is still unfamiliar or unclear to many, perhaps because of its almost taboo image. And yet the word is picturesque, dramatic, emotionally charged, and it means to produce a noticeable and durable improvement in performance, to turn around the trend of results from down to up, from not good enough to clearly better, from underachieving to acceptable, from losing to winning. It is a useful, visceral word, with overtones of purposeful action, even heroic achievement, that go with the American character.

Today every company has an industry group to which it belongs and to whose members it is compared. When a company, either as a whole or in one of its divisions or depart-

ments, is consistently performing below the average or midpoint in its industry group, then for that portion of its business
or for the total company its report card is below the average
for its class.

This is not illegal or shameful or despicable. But if it is a
fact it can either be allowed to continue or it can be recognized as an opportunity calling for special effort to raise performance above the group average. *It then becomes a turnaround situation.*

WHO WANTS TO BE BELOW AVERAGE?

There is nothing sacred about the average as a threshold of
underachievement. You can set it lower or higher. But it seems
that in our kind of society the fact that most of the members of
your group are doing better than you should cause the adrenalin to flow and start the inner voices saying, "For heaven's
sake, do something!" or at least "Hey, we've got an opportunity
for a turnaround!"

When Marshall McLuhan said "The medium is the message," he could have been talking about a turnaround, where
the medium can be the threshold for a turnaround movement.
Because once you accept the average (or medium) as a practical minimum for acceptable performance in a dynamic economy, it follows that about half of the companies are candidates for a turnaround, and that the facts are giving their
managements a mandate to begin gearing up for a significant
upgrading of performance.

Of course, we can't all be above average. But the powerful
point is this: Should professional management become *re-
signed* to continuing below-average performance as a way of
life? Or should management accept the average as a check-
point that triggers remedial action wherever results fall below
average. More than that, it *expects* the executive faced with
such a challenge to get into action or if he is blocked to get out
and go somewhere else.

*The fact that you are reading this and are interested in
learning about turnarounds, suggests that you belong in the*

*latter category of opportunity-oriented, action-minded busi-
nessmen. Welcome to the challenging and rewarding world of
turnarounds!*

ARE MANAGERS MORE RESIGNED THAN RESIGNING?

The recognition level on turnarounds is appallingly low.
One of the leading and widely accepted management associations recently sent out a brochure about a seminar on turnarounds for top management to a list of almost 40,000 American companies. The brochure presented the material very
well, saying that a management climate of high risk and volatility requires a CEO to be prepared to take prompt and deci-
sive action in a turnaround situation, and the seminar was
designed to help them recognize and develop potential turnaround opportunities for their organization. This mailing produced a surprisingly small turnout, less than a third of the
expected response, a telling identification of American management's blind spot on the turnaround question.

In a later chapter we will see how this turnaround myopia
is sapping the vitality of American industry, with the result
that we have much to be concerned about in the international
posture of the U.S. economy.

INSURMOUNTABLE OPPORTUNITIES

And so it seems that the plentiful opportunities we are confronted with in business are all too often insurmountable, as
the immortal comic strip character, Pogo, said. And the reason, he points out, lies in ourselves.

2

What's in It for Me?

A man's reach should exceed his grasp, or what's a heaven for.

—Robert Browning

WHY STICK YOUR NECK OUT?

You are a senior manager with responsibility for three divisions. The overall results of one division are somewhat below average in the industry. But nobody is really pressuring you to do anything heroic about it. There are plenty of reasons going back into the history of the company for the present situation, and you have two other divisions that are doing very well.

Why not leave well enough alone and concentrate on the good divisions? Wouldn't that be accentuating the positive? Or perhaps, at the psychological moment, you might put in a request for another division and get rid of the underachieving one.

PLAYING IT "SAFE"

The scenario described can be thought of as playing it safe, avoiding conspicuous risk. Because if this manager were to come on strong for a turnaround of his weak division, launch a bold program with topside approval, and then nothing much happened, he might expect to wind up in the company's bad books.

This point of view could not be more wrong. In a competitive world playing it "safe" — avoiding bold action involving risks — amounts to passing up the opportunities that bring the big rewards. For the manager who wants to grow, this kind of "safe" playing is just too *dangerous*. In competitive business the ostrich is an endangered species.

THE ENTREPRENEURIAL TYPE, GOLDEN BOY OF INDUSTRY

Risk taking is the lifeblood of business, a world where "nothing ventured, nothing gained" is literally true. When the annual reviews come around, top managements go through mountains of figures and facts, but what they really retain in their heads are the few instances where someone has built a successful product, conquered a difficult market sector, solved a deep-seated deficiency — all of which is part of improving performance and turning an operation around. The manager who has achieved a turnaround, big or little, becomes a man with wings on his heels. In well-managed companies, this type of entrepreneurial talent is apt to lead to the front office.

THE RISK TAKERS

All too often, however, companies in search of top management have to look outside and use high-powered search firms to find these skills. Again, what they are looking for is the individual who has in his résumé evidence of turnaround achievements, not someone who has maintained a respectable status in a prominent company by talking a good game and staying out of trouble, but someone who did indeed stick his neck out. Unfortunately the builders and risk takers are hard to find.

What if the enterprising, bold approach does not succeed? The manager who is hungry for turnaround opportunities will still do far better than his play-it-safe colleague, even if he fails occasionally. High-achieving businessmen know very well that the path leading to the heights of achievement has occasional potholes.

THE TURNAROUND: SCORECARD AND PASSPORT TO GROWTH

What it takes to set the stage for a turnaround are high standards, a freedom from self-delusion and defensiveness, and an appetite for challenges, accompanied by energy and determination—a tall order perhaps, but not any more than it takes for achievement in a healthy free-market economy.

Far from being seen as a calamity or disgrace, the turnaround opportunity should be recognized as a normal part of everyday business life. A manager's purpose in life is improvement. Therefore, if he wants to get ahead, he must seek out and tackle turnarounds, considering them the most creative and exciting part of his work.

Turnarounds, big and little, become the scorecard of a manager and his passport to a bigger job. When an executive is interviewed for a key position, the most meaningful inquiry is apt to center on where in his career he has been able to improve parts of his business, to turn bad situations into good ones.

The heroes and builders of American business have been the men who brilliantly managed turnarounds. Turnaround is just another word for opportunities, to be embraced not shunned. They are the seeds of growth for both the company and you.

3

The Size of the Challenge

Victory has a hundred fathers and defeat is an orphan.

—John F. Kennedy

MORE SUPPLY THAN DEMAND

Let us accept that of the fourteen million business firms in this country, the seven million or so that are performing below their industry group average are possible turnaround situations. What an enormous reservoir of potential improvement challenges American management! No one knows what fraction of these have been recognized as such opportunities and identified for a turnaround program, but it is undoubtedly a small part of the total.

That is not all. In addition, there are even more subsidiaries, divisions, and departments of companies performing below industry group average and hence asking for a turnaround. And these partial turnaround situations exist in almost every large company, even those at the top of their industry. *So our competitive, free-market environment generates an inexhaustible supply of turnaround opportunities, accompanied by low recognition of their existence and low action drives toward making the most of these opportunities.*

FEW PUSHOVERS

Major turnarounds are not easy to accomplish, nor are they quick. Business history does not abound with plentiful samples of successful major turnarounds. To begin with, many strike out because of too long delayed recognition of the need for a turnaround. When earnings declines go on for years, the management is not happy, but all too often it limits itself to halfway measures. The human dynamics in such situations are against facing up to the deficiencies of the management and favor going along with the existing team, hoping for improvement through palliatives.

Eventually the company may come to accept its mediocre position in its industry and stay grooved on that level. Occasionally, after continued losses, the board of directors may step in under the leadership of outside directors or the banks and change the top management.

Failing that, the company's history may enter a new chapter: Chapter XI.

Chrysler is an example of an eleventh-hour vigorous attack on a turnaround need. The symptoms were there for a number of years, but it was not until the company became a survival problem that it finally faced up to the turnaround. Now even the best possible turnaround program is skating on thin ice, whereas if it had been begun before the company's financial situation became precarious, it might have been a different story.

SUCCESS STORIES

American Broadcasting Corporation, Gould Inc., Olivetti, Volkswagen, Hercules, Litton, Kresge's are all examples of successful large company turnarounds, each led by a CEO or equivalent with his eye firmly planted on the turnaround goal: Fred Silverman of ABC, William T. Ylvisaker of Gould Inc., Carlo DeBenedetti of Olivetti, Tony Schmucker of Volkswagen, Alexander Fortunatus Giacco of Hercules, Inc., Fred O'Green of Litton Industries, Harry Cunningham of K-Mart.

Each of these winners has its own scenario. But they all have one thing in common: early recognition of the need for a turnaround posture. Sad to say—and it is one of the underlying concerns about the vitality of the American economy— early recognition of turnaround problems is all too rare in American business. And when turnaround myopia or blindness exists it eventually leads to the Penn Centrals, the W. T. Grants, and the thousands of corporate failures that do not make front-page news.

IT TAKES TIME

The time span of a turnaround begins with the recognition of the need and the opportunity, and continues with the development of a total program of action, which in time leads to the achievement of consistent performance improvement and an upgrading of position in the industry. This kind of reconstruction generally cannot be achieved overnight. It is sometimes possible to go into an underachieving company and hype the earnings for what might give the appearance of a turnaround. And there have been examples of companies with sound underpinning but the wrong top leadership, which respond dramatically to the entry of a new leader.

WORSE BEFORE BETTER

But in the main, the causes of prolonged underachievement in a company are deep-seated and spread throughout the fabric of the business. To change these soundly and to build a new winning way of life requires and deserves plenty of

time. In most cases a company needing a turnaround is on a
declining trend in earnings, and when the turnaround program begins the earnings continue downward for a while.
Moreover, some of the necessary ingredients in the turnaround program may cause a temporary drop in earnings to
lay the groundwork for solid future performance.

We must recognize, therefore, that most major turnarounds take about five years to get through the tunnel and
move onto solid ground. A typical profile of a major turnaround would be: one to three years to bottom out, then two
years of improved earnings taking the company toward its desired level of performance.

4

America's Turnaround Needs

Humility is a disgrace.

—V. S. Prichett

OVERSEAS COMPETITION

What a company can and should do about its turnaround in its industry is one thing. But American companies as a whole have something else to worry about. Comparing themselves with their industry group may no longer be enough, because much of American industry is slipping in the international competitive lineup.

In 1968 a book appeared in France that made a deep impression on the international business community. *The American Challenge* by J. J. Servan-Schreiber had as its thesis the point of view that America's secret weapon was its unique body of management skills and its development of a corps of world-champion professional managers that had produced the widespread economic conquest by American multinational companies.

THE NEW CHALLENGE TO AMERICA

In the years since 1968 the wheel has turned almost 180 degrees, and today the main thesis of Servan-Schreiber's book is outmoded. Europeans and Japanese in droves have long been getting M.B.A.'s at America's best schools of business administration. Their businessmen have been attending American management seminars, helped along by the establishment of numerous management courses abroad by business schools and management associations. As a result, professional management today is a way of life in most of the top-drawer companies in Europe and Japan, and the American businessman can find much that is stimulating and innovative when he visits those countries.

Most dramatically, the Japanese have turned around their industries in the last two or three decades from being cheap-labor copyists into innovative and dominant world-class competitors in capital-intensive and high-technology fields. Their weapons have been long-term planning supported by three-way collaboration among industry, banking, and government; powerful and long-range commitment to research and development; and strong employee motivation and company loyalty through lifetime job security and group participation in management.

A Japanese product once was tolerated by the American consumer as a cheap knockoff of the real thing. Today it *is* the real thing, engineered with state-of-the-art new features and manufactured on a level of quality control that we envy. Even in a field where American ingenuity pioneered, like small computers (expected to grow to a $9 billion business by 1985), we are bracing ourselves for the arrival of stiff Japanese competition, which is expected to capture a third of the market by 1985. This will be accomplished not with lower prices alone but with technological and design innovations. Result: The

American company now at the top of its industry may soon find itself demoted by international competition.

AMERICA AS A
TURNAROUND CANDIDATE

All of which suggests that America itself is in need of a turnaround. Here is the evidence: (1) our share of the world's manufacturing exports has been falling dramatically; (2) our real GNP growth no longer is above the average of the developed countries; (3) we have a lower rate of investment than the more dynamic foreign countries; (4) our productivity per man hour has fallen below that of our aggressive foreign competition; (5) our famed entrepreneurial drive is lagging and we have not moved as boldly into new techniques such as robotics as have some international competitors; and (6) labor's motivation and quality control are not up to the best international competitive standards.

For these reasons we have suffered the national embarrassment of seeing our long-time champion automobile industry in disarray and reeling before foreign competition, which has beaten us in recognizing the needs of our own market and outdone us in manufacturing efficiency. The core of our industrial bone-structure, the steel industry, is suffering from a similar illness, and other industries are not ashamed to clamor for government protection against foreign competition. Add to this the ravages of recession, and there can be no doubt that turnaround needs are accelerating throughout the U.S. economy.

NATIONAL HUMILITY OR AMBITION

The uneasy feeling has seeped into our consciousness as a people that we are no longer what we used to be in the world economy. After generations of taking it for granted that we are number one, we are shocked into the realization that our international primacy has eroded both in the economic and political fields. Surely the dramatic shift in the 1980 presidential election tells us that the public is aware of our underachievement and wants a turnaround.

If we are to cure our tired-blood symptoms and turn our situation around to the kind of American international economic leadership that prevailed for generations, it will require the growth of a turnaround mentality in big and little situations throughout our industries. If our vast opportunities are not to be insurmountable, we will have to develop to a high degree early awareness of turnaround challenges in all their forms, the skills and techniques to make the most of them, and a hunger for high achievement.

5

Turnarounds:
The Art of the Possible
in Business

We are such stuff as dreams are made on.
—Shakespeare

To summarize, this is what this book is all about:

1. *Raising the recognition level* of turnaround situations; helping the business navigator to scan constantly the competitive horizon, looking for areas where he is functioning below par for his industry, so he can seize upon and profit from valuable opportunities.

2. *Removing the stigma* from turnarounds and replacing it with the awareness that they are a normal, everyday part of business management, an executive's best friend, and the key to personal, company, and national growth.

3. *To help a manager achieve a successful turnaround* and deal with the deep-seated and complicated obstacles that beset his path, this book presents a turnaround blueprint born of proven, battle-tested ideas supported by long experience and observation of what helps industry's champions.

BLUEPRINT FOR TURNAROUND

The prescription has six components, metaphorically entitled: THE WILL, THE VEHICLE, THE ROAD MAP, THE MOTOR, THE FUEL, and THE PILOT. These translate into the following:

Getting ready (The will)

Special

Ten enemies of a turnaround, including the special problems of the family business; six preconditions; and sixteen underlying principles for a successful turnaround.

Building the team (The vehicle)

How to go about the complicated and difficult task of building the human resources of your business and coming up with a team that can win against competition. The entrepreneurial skills and turnaround-effective qualities to be sought, making the most of the existing team, gearing up for management development, and how to recruit high performers, rethink the organization structure, and manage the team for maximum effectiveness.

The power of bifocal planning (The road map)

Laying the foundation for a durable turnaround by building the planning function into a major force for getting results. Ten underlying principles for successful profit planning, applied to improving current performance, developing short-range and long-range plans, and the value of two-level planning and flexing the plan.

Turnaround strategies (The motor)

A guide to six key winning strategies in trend marketing, segment marketing, product mix, selling and sales promotion, production, and finance.

Motivating the team (The fuel)

Building bottom-line effectiveness in the management of the team. How to achieve motivation through the proven techniques of participative management, management by objectives, performance appraisal, and the management of time.

Monitoring performance (The pilot)

How to build effective management information systems as an aid to superior performance and an early-warning system for staving off problems. Awareness as a vital function of the pacemaker manager. The usefulness of the flow-through concept, and the vital role of the Chief Financial Officer.

A CALL TO ACTION

This book is dedicated to finding success in a vital and rewarding endeavor that is currently suffering from too much fear and failure, by describing the terrain to be covered and the various roads that lead to the goal. And since the turnaround is really a microcosm of the whole field of successful management, it amounts to looking upon the turnaround as *the art of the possible* as applied to business.

PART II

Getting Ready (The Will)

The reason why worry kills more people than work is that more people worry than work.

—Robert Frost

6

The Enemies
of a
Turnaround

*The Spartans do not ask how many the enemy
number, but where they are.*
                              —Agis, King of Sparta

If the mental blocks are out of the way, let us begin by getting to know some of the characteristics of underachieving
companies. An examination of the pathology will help us arrive at the treatment. Here are ten turnaround enemies.

THE REAR-VIEW MIRROR

Retrothinking management doing the things that worked
in the past but don't seem to work anymore. This is the most
frequent characteristic of troubled companies and it is
grounded in human nature. To continue what is successful is
natural, but the danger is that at some point along that path

repetition becomes habit-forming. Then what was once a well-thought-out course of action becomes an entrenched way of life. Probing, questioning, awareness of change all diminish, and the past moves into the driver's seat. The management is driving with its eye on the rear-view mirror.

ENJOYING LOW EXECUTIVE TURNOVER

LOW EXEC TURNOVER

In these days of mounting executive turnover brought about by the competitive search for managerial talent, the underachieving company will frequently be found to be "enjoying" low executive turnover. The management prides itself on not losing its people and on having a wealth of experience in its management, thanks to long-time incumbency. But this pride is suspect, because to the results-oriented observer the reasons behind this condition are all too clear and do not bring happiness. The sacred cows that inhabit such a company have gained the lasting affection not only of their own management but also of their competitors, who love them just where they are. And so there are few bidders for their talents and the search firms give them a wide berth. A company whose management team is loaded with number 2s and 3s on a scale of 10 will not be troubled by recruiters looking for number 8s. The "pleasant" low-turnover condition itself becomes the culprit.

LITTLE SELF-CRITICISM

C-AVERAGE

Another symptom of the underachieving company is the prevalence of a defensive posture in the top management. The style of the company is self-indulgent rather than self-critical. Business goes on day after day and people seem to be doing their jobs with little feeling that results are demanded. The team is playing the game for the game's sake, not to win. The company is like a well-born student at an Ivy League college whose family does not expect ungentlemanly high grades, and is perfectly happy with a well-mannered C average.

REGULARLY MISSING PLAN

As a result, performance is usually below plan, meaning that generally sales and profits fall short of announced expectations. It is rare to find a company that does not have a monthly plan of sales and profits, and it is equally rare to find an underachieving company where, if results over the last three years are tracked, it will have achieved these plans more than one or two months out of the year. This distressing fact receives little attention or publicity in company channels. What sometimes fills the vacuum is a plentiful supply of excuses.

A HOUSE DIVIDED

Another symptom in the pathology of the underachieving company is a poor flow of communications between the functional divisions of the organization. The sales division blames its troubles on the manufacturing division for failing to produce the right kinds of products. The manufacturing division is convinced that what the company needs is a decent sales force. Division heads spend a lot of their time assigning the blame beyond their areas of responsibility, at the same time keeping a close guard on their own authority and shutting out interaction between divisions as interference. The combination of hostility and low achievement leads to entrenched management enclaves with little constructive communication with others.

LITTLE DELEGATION

Instead of decision making being spread throughout the organization, it is confined to the top echelon. In spite of what job descriptions say, delegation is really considered dangerous. As a result, executives frequently operate at a level below their jobs. The supervisor tells his people what to do, rather than training them to make the decisions that belong to their job responsibility. They, in turn, work the same way with their subordinates.

MEETINGS AS AN AVOIDANCE TECHNIQUE

Another interesting characteristic is the prevalence of meetings. Much time is taken up with regular and specially called meetings that go on for hours. These meetings are full of animated statements of entrenched positions, with a low level of candor. There is little respect for people's time. Meetings are called on short notice with no announced agenda, and when a meeting is under way, additional people are often summoned on the spur of the moment. What are the results of all these meetings? Usually few decisions, plus a prevailing state of mind that the meetings themselves seem to matter more than agreed-upon action. In reality, meetings become an avoidance technique through which decision-shy managers, those characterized by a congenital fear of making a decision, can at the same time put off taking a stand and assuage any guilt feelings by what they consider to be thorough and democratic soundings of their associates' opinions.

CEO MONOLOGUES

Another variant is the dictatorial chief executive officer surrounded by submissive managers whose main objective is staying on the payroll by doing the boss's bidding. In this environment meetings tend to become monologues. Hollywood's predilection for this was summed up in Samuel Goldwyn's dictum, "I don't want any yes-men around here. I want everyone to tell me the truth even if it costs him his job."

Very Important

CRYING "WOLF!" TOO OFTEN

In a troubled company, the management is sometimes given to sounding dire warnings that are not accompanied by a program of action. People get used to hearing that calamity is on the way and yet nothing seems to be done about it. The management loses credibility and the people get used to purposeless grousing.

LACK OF BOLD ACTION

When decisions are made in a climate of underachievement, they are apt to be cautious and limited by fear of change. The timid philosophy of playing it safe has been ineffective and even dangerous for a long time, refuted even in ancient Rome by the saying, "Fortune helps the bold."

7

The Family Business

A man's enemies are the men of his own house.

—Micah

In identifying the obstacles to a turnaround, the family business has special problems that deserve attention.

THE LIFE CYCLE OF A BUSINESS

The business enterprise in our open system takes many forms, but looked at historically its typical life cycle seems to have three phases:

1. It starts out as an individual or family business.
2. If it does not do well in the competitive arena, it may ultimately be sold or liquidated, or more probably join the ranks of bankruptcies, which are now occurring at the rate of 35,000 a year. If it does do well, it grows,

and in our generation eventually "goes public": that is, it allows outside investors to share ownership of the company, the family usually retaining control.

3. After a generation or two, unless the family has been exceptionally prolific in managerial talent, the large family business, in its development of nonfamily managers, reaches the point where first the chief operating officer and then the chief executive officer jobs go nonfamily. The family remains importantly on the board of directors, but the company has made the transition to the status of a public company run by professional managers. It has joined the ranks of such distinguished family companies as Dupont, Mellon, Ford, Anheuser-Busch, and Dayton-Hudson. Most of today's public companies have their roots in family businesses.

The reasons behind this evolutionary process in the growth of business enterprises are numerous. Here are five of them.

Is talent hereditary?

The major survival problem in a family business — and here it shares its dilemma with hereditary monarchies — consists of the abilities and qualities of the leader. The first entrepreneur who makes the business grow obviously has above-average skills, judgment, and drive. As the founder ages, the wealth and position wrought by success often begin to erode these qualities. The second-generation chief executive officer often lacks the founder's drive, but with benefit of better education and other advantages may take the business into expansion and modernization. As for the third generation, it is the exceptional family indeed that can muster the strength of leadership to maintain a dynamic competitive position in its industry. Inherited affluence and expanded interests tend to weaken the inheritance of the founder's drive and dedication to the business, unless the family makes a strong effort to combat this tendency, as the Rockefellers and a few other families have done so successfully.

Sliding standards and royalty

As a result, standards of performance begin to slide and the underachievement characteristics described in the last chapter emerge. As time goes on, a royal family syndrome may develop as members of the ruling family are addressed by the regal first name: "Mr. Robert, Miss Helen." The company becomes a social structure with class distinctions, where family members, after several generations of affluence, are the product of Ivy League education, world travel, ample trust funds, and cultivated tastes, accompanied by lowered preoccupation with the business. Circumstances begin to resemble the old English saying: "Who likes not his business, his business likes him not."

Sound management undermined

As the stage is now set, free interaction with the rest of the organization becomes difficult. The CEO does not think in terms of shared responsibility or wanted group participation, and decision making tends to be postponed. Family pride tunes out frank self-appraisal and with it the entrepreneurial thrust. The general mood is one of staying with things as they were, with little appetite for facing the hard changes needed to solve the problems of the company.

Nepotism

The sacred cow problem described in the last chapter is even more difficult in the family business because it relates to relatives. Very few such businesses have applied professional standards to the family members approaching jobs. The controlling fact is the family's right to run the business, and not the need of family members to win their spurs in their jobs like anyone else. And once nepotism seeps into an organization, results-oriented management withers away.

Recruiting obstacles

When such a family business decides to recruit management strength on the outside, it has to overcome the inherent handicap of its image as seen from the outside. The high-performance manager looking at such a company must have an answer to the big question of whether deep-seated conditions can and will be changed, and what the frustration level is apt to be. This is not to say that such recruiting cannot successfully be done. It can, but only if the company's leadership thoroughly understands the demands of the situation and is ready to make the tangible and intangible changes as well as the management commitments needed to turn the company around.

8

Preconditions for a Successful Turnaround

Discovery comes to the prepared mind.
—Louis Pasteur

We have taken a candid look at the enemies of a turn-around. They are not much fun, either to read about or to live with. But any sound cure must be based on a thorough understanding and recognition of the underlying pathology.

FIRST, TURN AROUND YOUR MIND

Before beginning to put together a comprehensive program for a company turnaround, its leadership must, as a precondition for success, undergo a mental turnaround, a radical change in the approach to the running of the company, affecting all the components of the coming turnaround program.

Here are the main preconditions on which to launch a turnaround:

1. Management determination

Since turnarounds are not easy, plentiful or quick, it is essential that the minds of top management be tuned up to the pitch needed to play the piece. With a firm resolve management must stand ready to pay the price of a turnaround by being willing to do the things outlined in this book, some of which will be difficult, even painful. Dealing with deep-rooted conditions calls for strong medicine.

2. Dispose of the enemies

Having taken a look at the turnaround enemies, we must be prepared to defeat them. We must be ready to dig ourselves out of habit-ridden grooves, to remove incorrigible underperformers, to let in the fresh air of participative management, and to move the business toward first-rate professional standards.

3. General parameters of the shortfall

We must quantify our overall performance shortfall so that we begin with a clear understanding on the part of all concerned of the distance between us and our objectives. For example, if sales growth has been running at about 2 or 3 percent a year and the industry average is 7 or 8 percent, then a first requirement is to recognize the company's need of quantum change in its rate of growth that would bring it toward double-digit annual sales increases. Similarly, it is helpful to agree at the outset as to where we are on the industry performance curve on profit margins, expense, pretax profit percent to sales, return on equity, and the debt to asset ratio, so that the general parameters of our shortfall are understood and recognized.

4. Identify underlying causes

As part of the approach to a turnaround, it is well at this stage to identify the underlying causes of the shortfall, not in great detail, but the key factors that have brought us to where we are. These will, of course, be amplified and documented as we get into the architecture of our turnaround program in later chapters.

5. Establish standards and timetable

Armed with the foregoing, and before we begin to shape the program, we must be careful to screen out unwarranted optimism and pie-in-the-sky euphoria. One of the most defeating developments in this kind of situation is a general bandying about of the word *turnaround* prematurely, before management resolve is fully matured and the groundwork for action laid. This is what John Kenneth Galbraith called "the lethal disease of being right too soon." Nothing will kill our undertaking quicker than destroying credibility by making campaign promises of a turnaround backed by hope alone. Therefore, there should be thoughtful agreement on the general standard of performance that will be the company's objective and the general timetable for its achievement. Durable turnarounds are rarely accomplished as quickly as expected. The more deep-seated the company's underlying problems, the longer it takes for a cure. Even in the best-managed turnarounds, things will often get worse before they get better, because the remedial steps may temporarily have a negative effect that is unavoidable as part of the transition.

6. Milestone communication to the organization

When this is done and the top management's state of mind is solidly on the track, we are ready to make a milestone announcement to the entire organization to the effect that the company will be taking a new direction, that a comprehensive renewal program will occupy center stage for the next few years, aimed at moving company performance ultimately into the upper echelon of the industry, where it belongs. This requires an unusual communications effort by the CEO, usually an all-day session with the entire executive staff. It should produce widespread understanding and commitment, as well as a sense of urgency and a general belief that the company will achieve its mission. Experience has shown that the resultant surge in morale and will to win have a positive effect on results almost at once. In all this communication the word *turnaround* should be avoided. What is needed is a program of action, not a promise. Turnaround talk at this stage casts the leadership in the role of would-be miracle men, and invites cynicism. *The label* turnaround *belongs on the finished product when the achievement is recognized and applauded by all.*

9

Sixteen
Key Principles

Man is not made for defeat.

—Ernest Hemingway

Let us assume that we now have the turnaround mentality backed with a high-intensity will to achieve our difficult objectives. Before we move into our new environment, we can use some compatible mental furniture in the form of battle-tested key principles with a history of success. Some of these may sound obvious, but unfortunately the obvious is too often a victim of benign neglect, even when it has much to offer.

THE MAGIC QUESTION

High-performance companies like to let the customers run their business. That means they begin with a clear picture of the customers targeted, and then cultivate an intense awareness of how each customer feels about everything the company does. The magic question is: *Why should the customer buy from me?* It should be asked continually in every part of the business. The magic of the question is that it forces constant reevaluation of your competitive position in the customer's mind. Applied to each company product, the magic question brings answers that keep management aware of where the growth potentials are, where there is slippage, and, in total, what the marketing posture is in the competitive arena. There is nothing startling or new about this little-used idea, but there is a guaranteed payoff for any CEO who makes the magic question a widespread habit in his organization.

THE PERPETUAL CONTEST

In our competitive industry environment, each member of your team should be thought of as being in a contest with his counterparts on your competitors' teams. Whatever the job, if your man is a number 3 on a scale of 10, and your competitors are 7s and 8s, there is no way that your company can be the winner in that area. This principle suggests you develop an industrywide yardstick in appraising your people and a heightened awareness of each team member's opposite number in the competition.

GROWTH A MUST

You can get temporary improvement in earnings in many different ways, but in the long run there is no permanent upgrading of performance without significantly better sales trends. This is especially true in an inflationary environment. The correlation between consistent earnings growth and share-of-market growth bears out this principle. In a turnaround situation, therefore, you must move toward better-than-industry average sales growth. In effect, you must *gain share-of-market from your competitors* in order to pass them in earnings improvement.

SPOTLIGHT ON RESULTS

Another characteristic of high-achieving management is that is is *results-oriented*. It starts with the CEO convincing all layers of management that the team is out to win and will live by the score, with each team member being responsible for his results. Bottom-line responsibility is spread down into middle management ranks, and bottom-line results receive great emphasis and wide currency throughout the organization. Results achievement then becomes the key to individual advancement as well as company growth.

THE POWER OF PLANNING

More and more, superior performance begins with superior planning. In the technology of management, the planning function has grown dramatically in its impact on performance, both short range and long range. The cause-and-effect relationship of planning skills to results is so strong as to make it a competitive factor in any industry. Short-range achievement of plans should not be allowed to overshadow the vital importance of long-range planning. A durable turnaround cannot be achieved without a five-year road map to provide guidance for the management in its long and difficult mission.

USE YOUR COMPETITORS

Make a real effort to get as much detailed information as possible about your competitors' performance. There is no better group motivator toward bold action than the cold facts about how your competitor has outstripped you in a segment of the business. By using this information to advance your own ball on the field, you are *putting your competitors to work for you.*

CORRECTIBLE ERRORS

Everyone is expected to make mistakes, though not to re-peat them. As with one's children, the worst thing an executive can do is harp on his people's errors. The better way is to make the mistakes productive by recognizing their great value when properly used as a stimulant to performance improvement. By keeping an inventory of correctible errors each team member builds a storehouse of opportunities for improvement. In to-tal, correctible errors can become an important asset of the business not shown on the balance sheet.

SUCCESS AS AN ENEMY

In the necessary pursuit of success, remember that success itself can be destructive. For reasons inherent in human na-ture, success has often led to the demise of once-important companies. A manager who has enjoyed three good years in a row can change before your eyes. He now knows the answers and seems to develop a growing hearing defect when it comes to listening to what others have to say. Complacency marches in to take the place of questioning, self-criticism, seeking fruit-ful change. Before long he becomes vulnerable to the upstart competitor who is pursuing success with open-end vigor. The same process is at work in a company as a whole, as we see even long-time industry leaders like General Motors and Sears Roebuck, after years of being the rich boys in their industries, suffering from late recognition of fundamental changes in cus-tomer attitudes. Indeed, just as the individual who retains humility and an open mind after great achievement and wealth is a rare bird, so it can be said that few industry-lead-ing companies are able to stay young and hungry mentally for very many years, learning to remain insulated against the un-dermining effects of the success syndrome.

GOODMAN'S LAW

This nomenclature derives, with apologies, from associates exposed to the admonishment that in our imperfect world long experience tells us that, never mind where, when, or what you are doing, *one in four things is apt to go wrong.* So that if in "the best-laid schemes o' mice an' men" one in four things can be expected to go "agley," you had better be prepared for this and put it into your planning. If you want your program (or rescue mission) to succeed against all possible odds, you build in a substantial margin of safety: needing thirty without fail, set it up for forty.

MANAGING CHANGE

Pursuit of growth requires bold action, but always tempered by a sensible appraisal of the risks. Therefore:

1. Avoid bold moves in areas of the business where you are weak; *expansion from weakness is dangerous,* often fatal.
2. If it is a big change involving hard-to-measure risks, *test it in a small part of the business,* and when the pilot operation works, move ahead on a broader front.
3. The soundest *growth is organic,* that is, related to the nature of the organization, its strengths, natural tendencies, and characteristics. This does not rule out bold departures, but they shuld be made only after deep consideration and research. Spastic change can be ruinous.

AUTHORITY VERSUS INITIATIVE

In a company where people often speak of authority in relation to job performance, it usually reflects a narrow, restrictive environment that discourages initiative. If you want initiative in the pursuit of objectives, *authority* is a bad word because it becomes an excuse for turning off energy, of foregoing an opportunity to move toward a constructive goal simply because the activity is not in your job description and you could not be blamed for *not* doing it. *Management is getting results through people,* only some of whom report to you. When you persuade your boss or others not under your supervision to do what you want them to do, you are "managing" them. In a high-achievement company a great value is put on initiative, and therefore managers are encouraged to have influence beyond their officially defined authority. To make this happen requires persuasive skill, modest demeanor, and tact, but its encouragement can greatly accelerate a company's achievement pace. A good maxim for the team member is *"Think above your job, behave below it."*

DELEGATE BUT DON'T ABDICATE

The effective manager has a multifaceted leadership role that includes direct supervision of the people reporting to him and a constructive awareness of how lower levels in the hierarchy are doing. Don't be a prisoner of your organization chart, insulating yourself against contact with different levels of your pyramid. What is known as *skip-level communication* involves a top executive's skill in keeping in touch with, inspiring, and monitoring people in middle management without undermining reporting lines.

HOW VERSUS WHAT

What you do is important, but how you do it deserves just as much thought and effort, because it can make or break the project. Too often the general concept of any undertaking gets most of the thought, the execution less. Our federal government has provided all too many examples of the miscarriage of well-meant projects through inadequate performance skills.

In today's fast-moving environment, cultivating state-of-the-art professionalism in business logistics and methods pays off handsomely.

ACTIVITY VERSUS ACHIEVEMENT

"Don't confuse activity with achievement" is a useful maxim that is unfortunately not enough observed in the ominously growing public sector. When results orientation is weak in a business, management's consciousness tends to be filled with *process* instead of *goals*, and this is reflected throughout the organization. As a result, sincere and dedicated people can be very busy at work that ends up in little achievement. Working *smart* means more than working *hard*.

PARTICIPATIVE MANAGEMENT

Over the long pull, given equal talent, participatively managed companies do better, handle management succession more smoothly, and retain their vitality longer than dictatorially managed companies. Advances in the behavioral sciences applied to business have thrown much light on the dynamics of leadership and teamwork and are an important resource for the professionally managed company.

SCALE OF 10

Even before Hollywood gave us Bo Derek as a 10, the use of a scale of 10 in quantifying appraisal of performance, individual potential, and, in fact, anything measurable, has proven extremely helpful. When someone says "good," there is no way of knowing whether this means about the best that can be expected or a midpoint beneath "very good" and "excellent." The scale of 10 will be widely used in this book, and is heartily recommended as a painless way to gain precision in communication. Psychologically it is one of the best movers since the wheel.

PART III

Building the Team (The Vehicle)

I don't make my figures if you don't make your figures.
                    —David Mahoney

10

Begin with Management

There are no bad orchestras, only bad conductors.

—Anonymous

TURNAROUNDS REQUIRE
MANAGEMENT CHANGES

Just as you must break eggs to make an omelet, the inescapable fact is that management changes are needed to produce a turnaround. The very definition of management—getting desired results through people—puts the onus on management for not getting the results. There is no way of getting around the fact that the major cause of continued malfunction in a business is management inadequacy.

45

YOU CAN'T DELEGATE
UNDERACHIEVEMENT

The manager who says, "My problem is the people I have to work with; I know what needs to be done, but I don't have the people to do it," is a workman blaming his tools.

Let's analyze the situation. The manager has articulated a course of action that has not proven successful, allegedly because of faulty execution. Well, leadership, whether of a large corporation or a small division, is *the art of getting others to do what you feel should be done.* If they are not doing it, it must be because (a) they don't want to, or (b) they are unable to. If it is (a) then our manager has failed in his leadership function of getting them to want to do it. If it is (b) then our manager has failed in appraising the capabilities of his people and by not replacing or improving by training those that fall short. If the replacing cannot be done with ideal speed because of personnel constraints, then the manager should have negotiated the best possible timetable in view of those restraints and have built this timetable into his action program.

In any case, it is clear that the lines of force lead straight to the manager and that in terms of the needs of a turnaround we must generally accept the old saying the "there are no bad orchestras, only bad conductors."

DISTINGUISH BETWEEN SYMPTOMS
AND CAUSES

The symptoms of the troubled company described above as the enemies of a turnaround, must not be confused with the causes of the company's predicament, anymore than the thermometer is making the room hot. What we are looking for as the underlying cause is *the thing that, if it were removed, would cure the problem.* And it is the very fact that the arrows point at management that has kept so many turnaround situations in the closet, with the door locked by management itself.

All too often management ducks the issue by trying to get better results through replacing subordinates. This is like protecting a weak backhand in tennis by running around it with the forehand. It evades the main issue and is doomed to eventual failure because it perpetuates a weakness rather than correcting it.

Moreover, *better people poorly led may do worse than average people under gifted leadership.* Put a high-potential individual under a low-potential boss and you get frustration that puts a drag on performance. In contrast, an outstanding supervisor raises performance above normal or expected levels, and can get superior results with people of average ability.

WANTED: THE ENTREPRENEURIAL MANAGER

Therefore, the first step in a turnaround, without which everything else is apt to fail, is the firm recognition that management must be strengthened, and that there is to be an end to wishful thinking, because Band-Aids don't cure cancers.

Admittedly this will involve a bold change of direction, and bring with it concerns about upsetting the organization with new faces and a barrage of changes. There are two answers to this: (a) it is the price you have to pay for getting out of the morass of underachievement, and (b) if you bring in the right new management there will be a surge of morale after the initial uncertainty. In troubled companies, the people are well aware of the shortcomings of leadership even though they may appear to be at ease with it. And there's no surer boost to morale than tasting group success after failure.

RECASTING MANAGEMENT

In recasting management, what we are looking for are skills that are in short supply, skills that make for winning the competitive battle, in short, the classic skills of the entrepreneur: an instinct for risk taking, sure decision making, the habit of leadership, and being at home with difficulty.

Usually such talent is scarce in an underachieving company, but if it is there it should be seized upon, because the risks of choosing in-house talent, even if it is not considered "ready" are less than going outside. First-hand observation on the job provides, after all, the most reliable picture of performance, Of course, there must be accurate appraisal of these talents, both inside and out, if we are to avoid going from the frying pan into the fire. Moreover, entrepreneurial skills are sometimes not exportable, meaning that a manager can be a peacock in one environment and a feather duster in another, as certain European acquirers of American companies have found out to their dismay.

QUALITIES TO LOOK FOR

In addition to the entrepreneurial skills mentioned, these are some of the turnaround-effective qualities to be sought in a manager:

1. A *good team builder* with the knack of finding people with stretch in them, and the ability to make these people grow through getting results.
2. A *sure hand on priorities,* the ability to manage time so as to get results in a difficult situation, and to avoid squandering energy by developing cures for which there is no known disease.
3. The *ability to handle failure* by putting it to work for him through exploiting the power of correctible errors.
4. *Intensity and urgency* to get to the heart of the problem and absorb enough details to plot a sure-footed course to the goal.
5. The ability to *set the right standards and motivate* his team toward their achievement.
6. The sensitivity to *work with the existing management* firmly but considerately and without causing them to

lose face. Where the manager scores high on this quality, he has been able to bring about a successful turnaround as chief operating officer nominally reporting to a family CEO, but, in fact, making the important and necessary decisions with the full support of the CEO.

11

Take the Measure
of Your
Present Team

The CEO appoints and disappoints his officers.
—a stockholder

THE RIGHT YARDSTICK

Having made the key decision that strengthening management is the vehicle to take you to your turnaround, the next step is an accurate evaluation of the existing team to determine with as much precision as possible where it needs to be strengthened. Given the perpetual contest between your people and their opposite numbers in the competition, what is called for is an evaluation of each team member on a scale of 1 to 10 in terms of the industry range of performance.

SIX EVALUATION SUGGESTIONS

This is really the first step toward building an eventual program of management development in the company. The care and thought put into this evaluation and the accuracy developed is bound to pay off in the soundness of the whole team-building effort of which it is the beginning. What is required are a number of key things:

1. In-depth *knowledge of competitive performance* at each job level. Starting with the job description of each team member, first visualize the four or five key performance objectives inherent in the job, and then assemble all available intelligence as to how the incumbent is performing on each of these in comparison with the best that could be expected in the job, as well as the known or estimated performance of the opposite numbers in the competition. For example, if we are dealing with a sales manager, movement in share-of-the-market this year versus last year would play a significant part in the rating. Obviously, confidential data is hard to come by, but there is a great deal of informal information available in any industry from the various levels of participants, including customers. The important thing is that this beginning team evaluation deserves exceptional effort to make it as complete and accurate as possible.

2. If necessary to fill out gaps in information, a special effort should be made to gather *input from search firms and consultants* who specialize in your industry and have accumulated facts and impressions about its cast of characters.

3. Obviously this special appraisal of the team must be a departure from past annual performance ratings, which, in a troubled company, are sometimes invalidated by defensiveness, favoritism, and inconsistency. What is needed here is *a new objectivity* that takes a fresh look at each team member's performance as well

as a professional consistency in the use of the same
yardstick throughout the organization.

4. There must be an understanding from the beginning
   that in this evaluation there are *no sacred cows,* and
   that past favorites, friends, and relatives will be rated
   on the same basis as all others.

5. It goes without saying that the most important source
   of *input* for the evaluation is *within the organization* itself. It needs to be gathered from both line and staff
   people who work with the team member, and the information needs to be tempered by the credibility of the
   source. People who are themselves unsatisfactory performers are rarely accurate evaluators of others. Conversely, where you have an above-average performer, if
   his outlook is not distorted by his own ambition, his
   evaluations carry weight.

6. An excellent source of candid, unslanted information is
   the *employee opinion survey.* This is a professionally
   designed questionnaire probing how employees feel
   about their jobs, their supervisors, the company, and
   the many other job-related factors that affect morale.
   The questionnaire can be tailor-made for the company
   or developed by the personnel department from readily
   available models. The forms are filled out on company
   time and are not signed by the individual, but the department or operating subdivision of the company is
   coded or otherwise identified. The management is
   careful to explain that this survey is meant to help the
   employees communicate to the company how they feel
   about everything relating to their jobs, and that to get
   the most out of it employees must be completely candid
   in their answers. If it is done well and covers both rank-
   and-file people and executives, an employee opinion
   survey in the early stages of a turnaround brings two
   benefits: (a)an immediate general boost in morale in
   response to the company's evident interest in how the
   employees feel, and (b) a mine of useful information
   about employee-supervisor relations that can be very
   helpful to management in appraising supervisors.

CEO ROLE

This important job of team evaluation cannot be done without the strong involvement of the CEO if it is a total company turnaround, or the executive in charge if it is a division. From the outset, unless the boss is fully committed to the turnaround in the eyes of all and deeply involved in the whole process at each stage, it will have little chance of success.

For example, if top management stays out of it and leaves the evaluation to the personnel department, two undesirable things happen:

1. The organization will feel that the boss has already written off the existing team because he will not devote the time necessary for his personal involvement in the review and evaluation. This is apt to weaken motivation and destroy confidence in the eventual success of the turnaround. And if some people are later released, top management will be seen to be ruthless and inhuman in firing people without having taken the trouble personally to get to know the facts.

2. In delegating this key function, top management is bound to have lingering questions about the accuracy of the evaluations later on.

PERSONAL CONTACT WITH CEO

Given the extreme sensitivity of this first stage of a turnaround, especially where the chief executive officer (CEO) or the chief operating officer (COO) has recently joined the company, it is important to provide plenty of one-on-one contact between each team member and the top man. This should be done informally and casually, preferably at a breakfast or luncheon, and the tone should be that the boss is interested in each team member and wants to know more about his problems and opportunities. What is called for is healthy communication, with the boss refraining from pressure or critical statements.

IDENTIFYING MANAGEMENT NEEDS

Once the evaluation of the existing team is done with the proper care and accuracy, it provides a basis for deciding what changes need to be made and where the opportunities are for strengthening the team. These can then be put in order of priority and dealt with in the light of available talent inside and outside the organization.

12

Strengthen the Personnel Function

Few great men could pass Personnel.
—Paul Goodman

MANAGEMENT-BUILDING HELP

We have begun our turnaround attack by recognizing that the major cause of underachievement in a business is management inadequacy, and that the first task is to strengthen management. It follows that in this difficult and crucial management-building process the chief executive needs all the help he can get, beginning with a strong and professional head of the personnel function.

The fact that all top executives get involved in personnel decisions should not obscure the need for high-level specialized competence in the personnel function, just as it is needed in the marketing, product development, and other key functions of the business.

REEVALUATE THE PERSONNEL JOB

In companies that need a turnaround, the personnel department usually has a limited role. Do they recruit people? Yes, but except for low-level jobs they have little influence on decision making. They collect candidates from search firms and serve them up to the operating executives who decide who gets the nod and what the compensation will be. In the eyes of the management, therefore, this personnel department is a kind of service bureau doing the necessary tasks of paperwork, government compliance, labor negotiation, and the whole gamut of personnel procedure. It is kept busy coping with all this procedural work, but its impact on the vital question of *management competence* in the company is negligible because the assigned role is passive and not active.

NEEDED: A MANAGEMENT BUILDER

We must recognize early on that a two-fisted number 8 personnel executive whose major responsibility is management building is a vital part of a successful turnaround. This concept has been hindered by the proliferation of routine work in today's personnel function, and these demands too often have inhibited the more important creative side of professional personnel management. Just as the marketing function requires creative thinking about developing share-of-the-market, and the product development function calls for insight and imagination in coming up with products that will do well in the marketplace, the management development executive has the exciting, creative opportunity of molding the management team into a winning combination as a strong support system for the chief executive in the achievement of the company's objectives.

SEVEN THINGS TO LOOK FOR IN A PERSONNEL HEAD

Here are some of the requirements for an effective management-building personnel head, the kind that can play a key role in a turnaround:

1. In addition to a thorough grounding in the whole procedural side, which we need not go into here, the personnel head should develop a good working *knowledge of how the business functions,* what its major strengths and weaknesses are, and what kind of talent it takes to achieve top results in the various phases of the organization. He should never consider himself, as a professional personnel executive, foreign to the mainstream of the business, one who is not expected to understand how things work in the various divisions. To do well in his responsibility he should know enough about production work, research work, and sales work to develop an accurate grasp of the kind of human qualities it takes to succeed in these diverse responsibilities.

2. Through interviews in the field and work with the most competent search firms, he should develop informative *files on the outstanding performers among the competition,* their state of mind, and approximate compensation.

3. This should provide the background for judgment about the *profile of requirements for each major job* in the company as well as the range of compensation.

4. His *personal characteristics* ought to include self-confidence, warmth, enthusiasm, persuasiveness, and tact. They should not include timidity. The fainthearted personnel man, or one who keeps files of hedged recommendations to protect himself from blame, will never rise above routine levels in function and compensation.

5. Helped by his personality, he should be fearless about *taking strong positions with the chief executive* and the other pyramid heads. He should furnish independent thinking about casting people in management roles and should come up with imaginative selections that the boss would not have thought of. It goes without saying that he should resist being sidetracked in decision making and refuse to be relegated to a subservient personnel role.

6. He should *read widely in management literature* and know how to use the help of the behavioral sciences in management building.

7. Finally, he should *cultivate action skills* and develop a sense of urgency. These are needed to support his function as a top executive, but are not often found in people who have chosen a career in personnel work and have grown up in an environment that tends to be more contemplative than action-oriented.

SEVEN SUGGESTIONS FOR AN EFFECTIVE CEO TO WORK WITH HIS PERSONNEL HEAD

1. First of all, the kind of personnel executive we are describing should *report directly to the chief executive* as one of the five or six pyramid heads of the business.

2. The CEO should not have him in the job unless he *respects his judgment* and will not make personnel decisions without his input. The boss may find that he has a talented vice-president who has great instincts and an X-ray eye about people but who is not aggressive in advancing opinions and influencing decisions. In that case, the boss should work to develop action skills in his man, by requiring him to take positions and grow into a leadership role in the top management.

3. The head of the business should work with the personnel executive the way he does with an architect in plan-

ning a building: He starts out with a well-developed idea of what is needed but he *relies on the professional skills* he has hired to come up with the best possible design to achieve the objectives.

4. The boss should expect the personnel head to keep his *finger on the pulse of employee morale* in the company. The personnel staff should be circulating throughout the organization as a regular and accepted procedure. Through these informal contacts, supplemented by employee opinion surveys, it maintains accurate readings of the temperature of morale and provides early warnings of developing problems to top management.

5. The CEO should look to the personnel head for *counsel on compensation standards* and methods at all management layers in the company, including the top, based on competitive compensation levels and trends.

6. The CEO should expect the personnel head to *lead the motivational programs* of the company, especially Management by Objectives and Performance Appraisal. Developing the programs, selling them to the operating executives, installing them with the necessary training, and then monitoring how well they work, are all key personnel functions.

7. Although this is not as prevalent in management circles as it might be, there is much to be said about a final key role for the personnel head: that of the "*manager of the CEO*" himself. The chief executive has no one to report to except the board of directors, which is, for the most part, a ceremonial rather than managerial relationship. There is, therefore, no one to tell the boss how his management style goes over with the organization, whether there are a few chinks in his armor that need repairing, possibly with outside professional help, and generally to keep a professional eye on many things that may escape the awareness of a busy chief executive. The only question is whether the boss is smart enough to want this and big enough to encourage his personnel head to supply this valuable function.

13

Can People
Be Turned
Around?

*God changes not what is in a people until they
change what is in themselves.*

—The Koran

Once we have strengthened the personnel function as a
support system for the building of the turnaround management team, we are ready for the next question: To what extent
can we help the existing players to improve their game?

There are two components behind performance: *inherent
potential* and *form*, and both have to do with the mysterious
intangibles of personality and human interaction. How can we
in a business learn to navigate these fog-bound areas of the
psyche and arrive at our destination?

The answer is by making use of the state-of-the-art resources of the behavioral sciences, which, for a generation,
have been making steady progress toward answering useful

questions and providing valuable techniques in the field of management.

IMPROVING PERFORMANCE THROUGH PEOPLE SKILLS

We cannot remind ourselves too often that management means *getting results through people*. Therefore the manager's skill in interacting with others can make or break him. Whatever his inherent potential in intelligence, decision making, and creativity, it may be enhanced or destroyed by what happens when he faces his co-workers. *Mastering form* is the price of admission to superior performance.

THE DIMENSIONS OF MANAGEMENT BEHAVIOR

The behavioral sciences, in their application to business management, have come up with numerous approaches and techniques for identifying and influencing the various kinds of management style or form. For our purposes it will suffice to select one that is widely used with success, Dimensional Management Training as applied by Psychological Associates, Inc. of St. Louis. This firm has served four hundred large and small companies and has given seminars for developing people skills (Dimensional Management Training) to over 150,000 people.

WHAT MAKES THEM TICK?

The Dimensional Management approach moves us a giant step toward understanding the actors on the management scene by determining where each fits in a four-part grid characterizing management behavior. This technique is based on a good deal of psychological research in behavior classification over the past thirty years. The grid looks like this:

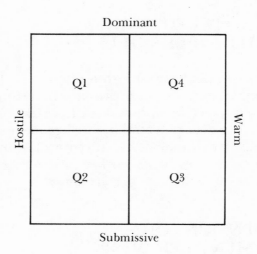

What follows is a boiled-down version of the essentials of this approach for the use of managers in a turnaround situation. For the full story, see the book *Improving Productivity Through People Skills* by Lefton, Buzzotta, and Sherberg, 1980.

The dominant manager is assertive in putting his ideas forward to control and influence co-workers; he takes charge, stays in charge, and *makes* things happen.

The submissive manager follows the lead of others, with little resistance to compliance or attempt to influence; he *lets* things happen.

The hostile manager is self-centered, with a low regard for others and, unresponsive to other people's feelings or needs, is cynical about their motives and doubtful of their abilities. His view of others is negative or pessimistic, not expecting much of other people or offering much of himself in return.

The warm manager is open-minded and his regard for others makes him sensitive and responsive to other people's feelings, needs, and ideas. He has an optimistic view of people.

YARDSTICK FOR UNDERSTANDING

The great value of this technique is that by combining these behavior characteristics into four quadrants, the whole confusing range of human behavior in business can be clarified and simplified so as to lead to understanding. Obviously, human beings are complicated and variable, and most people have elements of all four quadrants in their behavior. But what is important is to position the manager's major behavioral style in one of four quadrants: Q1, dominant-hostile; Q2, submissive-hostile; Q3, submissive-warm; Q4, dominant-warm.

Q1, dominant-hostile

The Q1 boss has a low opinion of his subordinates, feels he must get the job done by dictatorial methods if necessary, makes his decisions alone with tight control and little delegation. He exercises close supervision, one-way communication, and motivates his people with two-fisted realities. ("If you don't perform, you won't be here. Just do as I tell you, and I'll take care of you.") As a subordinate the Q1 is aggressive, demanding, unyielding, closed-minded, and in the pursuit of power will gain control by forcing his ideas and circumventing others.

Q2, submissive-hostile

The Q2 supervisor has a low opinion of his subordinates. ("Don't expect me to do better, considering the people I've got.") His strong concern is surviving in his job and he seeks a low profile. In his work he transmits instructions from above, appeals to authority, and handles his job with little direction, communication, or effort to motivate subordinates. The Q2 subordinate is aloof, guarded, neutral, noncommittal. Because he wants to stay on the job and keep out of trouble, his behavior is cautious and guarded.

Q3, submissive-warm

The Q3 boss feels that the main thing in running the business is to get along well with people, that subordinates work hard for managers they like, and that if the boss is congenial the results will somehow be there. He operates with loose controls, little real direction, sets vague, easily achieved goals; his delegation is not clear, and he makes popular decisions because of his belief in motivation through happiness. The Q3 subordinate, because he is eager to please, is overly friendly and agreeable, compromises and appeases, talks too much, and spends too much time socializing on the job.

Q4, dominant-warm

The Q4 boss is strong in his determination to run the business but believes the way to get the best results is by free and spirited interaction rather than unitary command. He feels that his people are goal-directed, their commitment comes from involvement, that their rewards and the company's come from superior achievement together, and that developing people is the sound way to build the business. As a result, he is a thoughtful delegator, involving subordinates in decision making. He encourages communication, open-mindedness, and candid self-expression. Without compromising his responsibility, he believes that mutually developed goals and a team motivated through involvement, understanding, and commitment are the way to get maximum results in the business. As a subordinate the Q4 believes in working with others to get results, is task-oriented, responsive, analytical, and questioning. His style is warm but frank and forceful.

The accompanying table shows a boiled-down picture of the four different management styles of the boss interacting with subordinates.

SUMMARY OF SUPERIOR'S STRATEGY TOWARD SUBORDINATES

Management Function	Q1 Dominant-Hostile	Q2 Submissive-Hostile	Q3 Submissive-Warm	Q4 Dominant-Warm
Basic Beliefs	Lazy — force, threaten	Lazy — do nothing	They will work — be friendly	Will work if committed — involve
Planning	By himself	Transmits from above	Loose, vague plans — if any	Strategic involvement
Controlling	By fear	Adhere to policy and what boss says	Permissive — human relations	Understanding of objectives
Decision Making	Makes decisions himself	Procrastinates, neutral	Selects popular alternatives	Chooses best, with understanding
Motivating	Coerce, threaten	Can't motivate	Affection	Their needs = company needs
Conflict	Cut off, suppress	Avoid	Smooth over	Confront and resolve
Communications	One-way	No-way	Partial	Two-way

65

TAKING YOUR Q

It is pretty obvious from all this that the Q4 is the good guy and the Q1 is the bad. This needs thoughtful amplification.

Actually, *the worst of the four is the Q3,* and his habitat is the underachieving company. He generates mediocre performance because he has low drives, an escapist mentality, and an absence of the will to triumph over obstacles. His garrulous conviviality is really a disaster, because it spreads time-wasting and happy unproductiveness among his people. He is also a charming fellow, enjoys a kind of popularity, and through long practice effectively tunes out the unpleasant from his consciousness. And so the Q3 manager can be the hardest of the four types to change productively. The organism of the popular and friendly underachiever rejects the results-oriented implant.

The next worst management style in its impact on results is the Q2, because of low drives, passive acceptance of the status quo, resistance to change, and fear of making any waves that would attract attention and possibly endanger his job security. But it is possible to get better results from a Q2 because of his strong desire to follow direction as compared with the fuzzy friendliness of the Q3. In the end, moving a Q2 or a Q3 toward constructive improvement is a continuing challenge to leadership.

We must be realistic about the Q1. He sounds like the villain of the quadrants, and we wonder if anybody good would work for him. And yet the fact is that there are more Q1s running businesses in America than all the other behavioral types put together, and the gifted Q1 often presides over the high-performance company. Indeed, in an emergency there is nothing like a competent Q1 to get quick results. More often than not, the entrepreneur who is good at starting a business, making it go, and developing it into a substantial operation is apt to be a Q1.

On a strictly pragmatic basis, *where the Q1 falls short is in the long run.* Q1s, by nature, are not good developers of people, although there have been some great entrepreneurial Q1s who, by their tough-minded adherence to getting results, were able to develop managers tough enough to make the grade in a high-performance environment and later go on to run big companies successfully. But for the most part, the Q1 boss tends to generate Q2s who are better at following than leading, and so when the Q1 leaves, for whatever reason, there is often a management succession problem.

Moreover, because so much rides on the health and energy of one individual, a dictatorially run company is no sounder than the boss's latest physical checkup. An old Q1 is therefore more of a problem, because neither the dominance nor the hostility diminish, but the energy and ability may.

THREE IMPORTANT STRENGTHS
UNIQUE TO Q4 MANAGEMENT

1. *The participative atmosphere brings out the best in the people* and group involvement builds confidence, determination, and healthy competitive effort, all of which help results.
2. As a by-product, all the *participants are learning people skills* and how to be successful managers themselves.
3. A key benefit is management continuity, an essential value that eludes many American companies, including some of the biggest. Q4-led companies rarely have to go outside for top management succession because their top management lives by team building and developing leadership. As a result, such companies have a staying power that produces consistently high performance in fluctuating economies. This in turn develops a long-range point of view about the business and a strong commitment to research and development and long-range planning as the company goes on to expanding horizons.

But this theoretically ideal management style must always beware of any weakening in the dominant thrust toward top

achievement. When that thrust is present, the Q4 company is
out in front, short range *and* long range.

Unfortunately, Q4 managements are, so far, in the minor-
ity. Professional observers of the American management scene
believe that top managements, classified by behavior characteristics, run something like this:

Dominant-hostile — Q1	65 percent
Submissive-hostile — Q2	10 percent
Submissive-warm — Q3	15 percent
Dominant-warm — Q4	10 percent (but growing)

The Q4 is largely an American phenomenon, growing
from tendencies toward openness, freedom, fair-mindedness,
and egalitarianism in the American character. The stronger
respect for authority and position that inhabit European and
Asian business is not as natural a breeding ground for the Q4
manager. The stunning successes of Japanese and some European managements are being achieved for the most part by
congenital Q1s working with historically obedient people who
have become powerfully motivated by company loyalty and
participative management techniques of the Q4 type.

AN AMERICAN WAY TO BEAT
FOREIGN COMPETITION

At this difficult moment in American economic history, a
tremendous opportunity lies in what behavioral science is telling us about management techniques. It is within our grasp to
use those lessons to develop more and more of the kind of participative management typified by the Q4, the kind of management that not only should come naturally to the American
temperament, but also produce high-level competence that
can last because it is based on group interaction and not the
solitary genius.

The Japanese, who have learned so well the lessons of
American management since the war, have built the strongest, most motivational group-involvement business environ-

ment that the world has yet seen. It is an outgrowth of several deep-seated factors in Japanese life, led by these two:

1. In spite of Japan's deep roots in authoritarianism, business leaders today have become convinced of the tremendous power of widespread participation in generating productivity and quality.
2. The deep-seated desire of the Japanese people to rise above limitations and to combine high motivation with confidence in and acceptance of their leadership. Thus, with largely Q1 and Q2 roots, they are achieving phenomenal results through business methods that have many Q4 characteristics.

HOW TO GROW PEOPLE SKILLS IN YOUR ORGANIZATION

More and more companies are availing themselves of behavioral science technology to improve their managers' people skills and thereby raise performance levels. To continue with the example used in this chapter, Psychological Associates gives seminars in dimensional management training both at their headquarters in St. Louis and at the offices of their clients. These five-day seminars divide the participants into teams of four or five, which, after general sessions, work separately as a team to learn about motivation and communication through role playing on closed-circuit television equipment. As the days go by, the candor becomes more and more complete, and the participant takes away a new understanding of the wellsprings of management behavior in his own case as well as in that of his teammates, plus a prescription for his own improvement.

After the individual managers have taken this DMT seminar, many companies take the next step of having an in-house seminar on teambuilding. What was learned about effective interaction between individuals is now broadened to help the whole team achieve *group* success in their various functions, thus raising the level of company performance.

CAN PEOPLE BE TURNED AROUND?

Deeply ingrained characteristics of personality are hard to dislodge. Yet experience in the fields of psychology and psychiatry have clearly demonstrated that *behavior can be changed* where there is a will to do so, spurred on by awareness of the sources of the individual's present deficiencies and by professionally guided training in replacing those deficiencies by desired behavior. The many companies that have tried to tap the resources of behavioral science through qualified professionals have found that coaching executives in people skills can bring impressive results to company performance.

A small percentage of managers may be so set in their ways as to be unchangeable. An equally small percentage will respond at once to a seminar and show a durable behavior change for the better. But for the rest the seminar provides a groundwork of awareness, which is the first step. The next steps can best be done in-house, with professional help backed up by top management endorsement.

The fact that an increasing number of high-performance companies are doing this as a way of life recommends it for a turnaround situation. Realistically it takes two or three years for a company to bring about a pervasive Q4 climate in its organization. But once captured this can become a powerful performance generator that brings the kind of muscle tone and general conditioning found in winning teams.

14

Testing
Individual
Potential

Don't be humble, you're not that great.
—Golda Meir

HOW GOOD COULD YOU BE?

We have seen how a business in search of improvement can help its people to do better by developing their people skills through the insights and training techniques available in the behavioral science field. There is another key area in which psychology has provided a valuable resource to business management, and that is in the testing of human potential.

HIRING THE UNKNOWN

It is no exaggeration to say that in American business most people are hired with inadequate information, and that, considering the cost to the company of an ultimate misfire in the hiring process, businesses invest enormous sums of money in personnel acquisition based on hope supported by hunch, on a brief history of past experience plus what can be gleaned from a set of interviews. And in a climate of high executive turnover and falling productivity, we can hardly escape the general conclusion that personnel acquisition as a form of business risk taking could use some improvement.

What top executive has not had the bitter experience, when having to replace a key team member, of wishing he had known a good deal more at the time of hiring about weaknesses later revealed. No one has counted the round pegs placed in square holes in our hiring process, but National Personnel Associates, a network of independent search firms, gives us an idea when they report that almost one out of three managers has a résumé making the rounds.

Clearly, then, although we can't expect to solve all the mysteries locked in an applicant's DNA, we need all the help we can get. Which is why there has been a dramatic rise in the use by American business of psychological testing as an aid to appraising individual potential.

MAKING TESTING WORK FOR YOU

There is no quick or easy way of doing it right. No test is of much use unless it qualifies in two respects:

Reliability, that is, consistency, so that similar people will get similar scores.
Validity, that is, that the test measures what it is supposed to.

It has been said that it costs some $3 million to develop and perfect a personality test of the highest current qualifications. Tests are generally beamed at throwing light upon two facets of the individual:

Technical skills that have a bearing on individual performance. These include intelligence, problem-solving ability, verbal reasoning, abstract reasoning, mental ability, and ingenuity.

Process skills and personality factors, including behavioral style, interpersonal skills, ambition, drive, stability, character, conscientiousness, and emotional control.

The tests should be administered and scored professionally and must be supplemented by thorough interviewing.

KNOW ITS LIMITATIONS

Helpful as it is, experience has shown that psychological testing is not infallible. It has been undergoing a slow process of improvement for two generations, and has reached the point where well-managed companies feel they are benefiting by using them, and the company in need of a turnaround should prudently resort to them.

Experience has shown, say the psychologists, that testing is at its most precise in measuring intelligence and aptitudes, with a track record of being right about nine out of ten times. Testing is also good on people skills, although less precise, being right on the whole seven or eight times out of ten. Where the tests are not very helpful, so far, is in the more mysterious realms of creativity, marketing skills, and taste.

PICKING THE TESTING FIRM

There are many firms doing psychological testing for industry all over the country, and you need to exercise some care in selecting one for your company. A good approach is to go to the psychology department of your local university for recommendations. Or talk to a successful, well-managed company not in your industry and find out what firm they use for testing their people. When interviewing possible firms be sure they have psychologists with Ph.D's from good universities, and get a list of their clients, so that you can call several of them for their candid appraisal.

Finally, it is important to see samples of the reports they have done on candidates tested. Beware of the well-written report that does an elegant job of hedging and avoids making a yes or no recommendation on whether the individual should be hired. The best reports will go out on a limb and project how the candidate will do in the job. No firm will bat a thousand, obviously, but the usefulness to the client company depends on the clarity and the frankness of their input. Essential in this process is the in-depth interview by the psychologist.

GETTING THE MOST OUT OF TESTING

Evaluating people is one of the most important and at the same time most difficult things a manager must do, where company success or failure may hang in the balance. To get the most out of psychological testing requires working closely with the testing firm people to see that they are focused clearly, not only on the individual under scrutiny but on the nature of the job for which he is being considered. The psychologist needs a good working knowledge of what it takes for success in that job, including interpersonal skills. You must also make it clear to the testing firm people that you require them to make clear recommendations for or against the applicant in the job as well as detailed comments on strong and weak points as he is visualized in that job.

Remember that testing is *a* tool to be used in selection, and not the sole determinant. The tool has been sharpened over the years to where it is now safe and productive to use, but it is not a substitute for the judgment and instinct of the members of management. In fact, a good psychologist will say that when management's gut feeling differs from the test, you had better go with the gut feeling. But remember that you did, and avail yourself of an interesting educational opportunity by rereading the testing report at review time a year or two later. This will tell you much about the firm you are using and about the divining powers of your own intestines.

15

How to
Recruit
High Performers

Too much of a good thing can be wonderful.
                                        —Mae West

GOING OUTSIDE

Let's face the fact that bringing in outside talent is generally a must in a turnaround. Losing teams don't often become winning teams without some new management and new key players. Sure, better leadership can get some improvement through skillful coaching and morale building. But the fact is top winning teams always have star players, so if you really want to move your losing team into the upper brackets in its league you must acquire some star performers.

If the turnaround is a total company, the directors may be seeking a new chief executive officer from outside the company. If it is a subsidiary company the search may be outside the subsidiary, but within the parent company's total structure. Unfortunately, there is often resistance to intercompany promotion, with the result that the search winds up outside the total company.

Of course, if in-house talent can be found to man key executive posts effectively, it is better than going outside, for a number of reasons: less risk, an internal morale boost, some saving in compensation, and possibly a faster start. But for the top leadership job in a turnaround situation, it is hard to fill the bill without going outside.

Here are some experience-tested pointers on how to recruit the hard-to-get top performers.

GENERAL PRINCIPLES

1. The first rule is to recognize that in this exercise *you are selling, not buying*. The old scenario of the trembling job seeker confronting the haughty reluctant employer is out of date and has nothing to do with the quest for people who are doing well where they are and not looking for a job.

Groucho Marx said, "I am not interested in joining any club that would have me," and we are almost in the position of not being interested in anyone who is a job-seeker. In fact, if a candidate already has his résumé out, we have to satisfy ourselves that it is for acceptable reasons and not because of lack of success on the job. With the present environment of mobility among managers, those acceptable reasons are more plentiful, but need careful probing.

2. In building the team, *work from the top down*. Recruit the general first so he can have the opportunity to pick his colonels, majors, and lieutenants. This is desirable as a principle, but in practice it is not always feasible, because finding the ideal general manager will take time, and there may be key posts in middle management that urgently require filling. In that event you must try to anticipate what the general manager's standards and preferences would be for his people, and when you are able to recruit him, he should have the benefit of the full picture on how and why his subordinates were

hired, with the understanding that after his arrival he will be in full control of the future development of his team.

3. *Learn from mistakes.* Recruiting is so far from an exact science that it should be a lifelong study for any general executive. Therefore, as you go along try to sharpen your recruiting acumen by reviewing past successes and failures in the light of how the recruiting was done: the search, the checking of past performance, the testing, and the interviewing.

4. The selling approach in recruiting means that you realize your job is to find someone who is a top performer and persuade him or her to leave the present job and join your company. Indeed, it is quite similar to any marketing effort where you are persuading the customer to stop buying what they have been and switch to your product. Therefore, part of your marketing approach to recruitment should include a variant of the magic question (see Chapter 9) Why should the candidate join you? You must have good and solid reasons in answer to this question, and as a good marketer be constantly thinking of the candidate's state of mind.

There are two parts to acquiring management from the outside: (a) finding the right candidate; (b) making the sale.

SEVEN SUGGESTIONS FOR FINDING THE RIGHT CANDIDATE

The search

In today's manpower environment, unless you are a *Fortune* 500 company with a large in-house executive recruitment operation, it will pay you to engage the best possible search firm. *Search firms have to be appraised like people*, based on their performance and potential. You are looking for a firm that has a good background in your industry and, therefore, extensive files on the movements of key performers over the past ten or fifteen years. Which means that they know who the good people are for a given job and whether there is a chance of interesting them in your opening.

The other key thing to look for in a search firm is superior ability to do *a thorough job of checking* a candidate's past performance and arriving at a convincing appraisal of his ability. This is an area of significant weakness in much executive recruitment. Companies are too easily sold on a candidate based on the bare-bones story in the résumé plus the impression made in the interviews. All too often this leads to frustration later on and that "if only we had known" feeling.

What then should you expect in the way of performance checking from the search firm? The answer is reliable information from informed, disinterested third parties. Again it depends on the quality of the firm's personnel files in your industry. In the case of your candidate, C, now with the X company, they will ideally know A, who until a year and a half ago was C's boss at X and has now gone on to head up Y company, as well as several co-workers of C's at X who have since moved to other companies and all of whom have reliable credibility. Very often the search firm will have placed one of these individuals in his present job, and is in an ideal position to elicit candor and objectivity.

It goes without saying that your personnel head, with his broader franchise as recommended in chapter 12, would understand all this and be good at motivating the search firm, but there is no subsitute for the involvement of the head of the business with the search firm on a frequent enough basis to get maximum results. Any firm is capable of a wide range of performance, depending on which firm member is handling the case plus the client's ability to motivate.

Your part is key

Even with the best of search firms, the role of your top executive and the personnel head is critical. Just as to build a great building you need the interaction of a great architect and an exceptional client, in working with a dynamic search firm your role is a vital one, for it includes imparting a clear picture of the needs of the job, the main qualities looked for in the candidate, a joint appraisal of the opposite numbers in the competition, plus a mutual exploration of the kind of compensation package that would help attract the desired candidate. Here again, even with the strongest of personnel executives, the CEO's involvement really pays off in heightened results.

Experience versus potential

Experience is important, but not as important as potential. In a turnaround situation what we should be looking for, especially in the top jobs, is the entrepreneurial type who can go into a new situation and make things happen, rather than one who has performed well in an organization without having been the prime mover in building a sector of the business.

A frequent mistake is requiring full experience in all facets of the job to be filled, and then coming up with a highly experienced mediocrity. And if you ask the question, Why should this highly experienced candidate take your job when he already has a big job in another company, possibly bigger or more successful than yours?, the only convincing explanation may be that he is not doing well and is concerned about his security. Therefore, given the fact that you are a company with problems, you have a better chance of attracting a good performer on the way up, one who has good experience in part of your job and whose growth may be blocked in his present situation. You would be offering him more rapid growth and a chance to achieve dramatic results, powerful reasons for attracting the entrepreneurial manager.

Flexibility

In general, then, avoid too rigid a recruiting profile. Some companies have built this up to almost governmental proportions, and in that kind of scenario one wonders how many of industry's great entrepreneurs today could pass personnel.

See for yourself

As part of the thorough checking of the candidate's performance, it is often a good idea, where appropriate, to visit parts of his operation and get a first-hand feel of his performance.

Perfecting the interview

Interviewing techniques vary according to the personality of the interviewer. But if we take a marketing approach to recruitment we should never lose sight of what is going on in the candidate's mind as the interview progresses. Candor on the part of the interviewer will produce matching candor in the candidate. People generally like to talk about themselves, and so it is a good idea to begin the interview by letting the candidate give you a capsule biography, punctuated by your occasional observations and questions indicating warmth and understanding. As the interview progresses, you can do more probing to learn about the candidate's values in life and in business, and his needs as he sees them. Many people are nervous in an interview with a possible employer, and while it is true that the strong characters are not apt to be nervous, it is a good idea to try to get across the thought that you and the candidate are both on the same side of the table because you have the same objective: to explore the possibility of joint success and achievement resulting in mutual satisfaction. To accomplish all this the interview cannot be brief or hurried. Three or four hours in one or more sessions is the investment in time needed for this important and fateful activity.

Professional testing

During the recruiting process, we often find our assessment of the candidate shifting from side to side. That's why professional testing is a valuable supplement. Nevertheless, respect your first impressions. They often turn out to be right.

MAKING THE SALE

Compensation

Candidates will often say that money is not the most important consideration. Don't you believe it. Other things are talked about more, but in the end your high-achievement manager has a strong desire to achieve the financial status commensurate with high peformance and to attain the net worth of a successful entrepreneur. For the sake of your turnaround, make up your mind to pay for excellence and not to allow rigid salary scales to keep out top talent. In the last decade we have seen an unprecedented explosion in the compensation of the stars in business just as in sports and entertainment. You must therefore have a realistic picture of compensation levels in your industry and be ready to go after your wanted candidate with a compensation package that will get his attention.

The word *package* is important too. Today's dynamic managers respond not only to incentive bonuses but to executive perks like clubs, cars, insurance, as well as various forms of stock options and other financial rewards of high performance. Naturally there are practical limitations in any particular situation, but the important point is that the difference between a number 9 performer and a number 6 will give the company a handsome return on investment for the extra compensation needed to attract the number 9. "The best is none too good" is a profitable maxim in turnarounds.

Titles

Titles are important to achievers. The potential entrepreneur has a strong desire to be a president or chairman, and very often that desire may be the reason why he can be hired, because that avenue may be blocked where he is. In middle management, a vice-presidency means a lot to someone who doesn't have such a title, and a "senior" or "executive" in front of the "vice-president" represents substantial psychic income that need not cost the company anything.

Who's my boss?

The reporting relationship also carries much significance to the candidate. The difference between reporting to the president and reporting to a vice-president is considerable. Moreover, in hiring middle management, thought should be given to the compatibility of the new recruit and his superior in the organization. Strength does not work well under weakness.

Where will I live?

One of the obstacles to be overcome in recruiting often is the change of location. Some cities have positive images and some negative. It is therefore important to invite the candidate's spouse to come for a weekend, and to do the necessary to provide a warm reception and promote a favorable impression of the community. Many an otherwise viable recruitment has foundered because of wifely objections. In this connection it is also important to expose the couple to the cultural resources of the community, which nowadays loom large in their impact on the life-style of the upwardly mobile executive's family.

16

Growing
Your Own
Management

*Why should we import so many third-rate
foreign symphony conductors when we have so
many second-rate of our own?*
                                    —Sir Thomas Beecham

WHY BUILDING MANAGEMENT FROM
WITHIN IS BETTER

The all-important management development process has
to be a blend of career building inside the organization and
outside recruitment for talent not available in-house. In the
typical turnaround situation it is to be expected that outside
recruitment, especially in the top team, will prevail. But in the
long run, a company will perform more consistently and have
more staying power if it does a superior job of building management from within, for the following reasons:

1. There is less risk of miscasting, because you know your
own people better.

2. It creates an atmosphere of personal growth, a big help in recruiting top beginner talent.
3. It results in better morale and team spirit.
4. You wind up with a more reasonable, balanced compensation level, less distorted by the high price of luring outside talent.

WANTED: RECRUITMENT-PROMOTION BALANCE

Your objective in recruiting beginning executive talent is to attract the best possible quality of material and then help them to grow and achieve fulfillment in the company. This will give you a positive image in recruitment circles and enable you to maintain a successful internal management-building program over the years. In order to achieve this an effort must be made to keep a judicious balance between demand and supply for beginning executive manpower. If you don't recruit enough good trainees it will mean that there will be some executive vacancies that cannot be filled from within, and you will have to go outside. If you recruit too many trainees there will not be enough promotions to keep them challenged and happy, resulting in discontent, defection, and loss of image for the company. The only way to achieve this balance is through careful planning.

FIVE-YEAR MANPOWER PLAN

What is needed is a road map covering immediate and future needs for management development, tied into the company's growth plans. These are the components:

1. An inventory of managers needed this year by division and department. Then, feeding in the plans for each sector of the business, a similar inventory for years two, three, four, and five.

2. Projected retirements, similarly by division and department.

3. Estimated losses of managers by company-initiated separation and individual-initiated departure, based on best judgment on the former and past experience on the latter.

4. Decide on approximate incubation time—how long it takes for the individual to be ready for promotion into each category of job—bearing in mind the various acceptable career paths. As illustrated in the chart below, line B (retirements) plus C (separations) plus next year's increase in line A (managers needed) minus line D (available replacement candidates in-house) tells about how many need to be recruited each year.

EXECUTIVE RECRUITMENT PLAN

Year	1	2	3	4	5
A. Inventory of managers needed	30	32	34	36	38
B. Retirements	4	4	3	3	2
C. Separations, quits, death/disability	7	5	5	4	2
D. Replacement candidates now in-house	4	3	2	1	0
Recruit (= B + C − D + next year's increase in A)	9	8	8	8	

BEGINNING RECRUITMENT IS COMPETITIVE, TOO

In the search for superior beginning executive material, it should be borne in mind that here again competition for the best is keen. In the long run, you are aiming for a self-sustaining management development program that will provide you with talent that can win in the competitive arena at all levels, including the chief executive officer, so that when the head of the company retires there is a great replacement available in-house plus a domino-effect series of promotions, and, in theory, the net recruitment is another trainee to put in the pipeline.

MARKETING APPROACH TO BEGINNING EXECUTIVE RECRUITMENT

Here are ten suggestions for successfully implementing *the marketing approach to beginning executive recruitment*:

Marketing aids

As ammunition for the campaign, a well-done recruitment brochure can be very helpful. It should tell a clear and positive story about the company and what it offers to an executive recruit as a career environment, including fringe benefits and personnel policies. Attractive company annual reports, press clippings, and financial analyst comments are all helpful in reaching the mind of the desirable prospect.

Define the market

Define the market in the sense of deciding at what schools and colleges the best material for your company is to be found. In any company there is a range of innate talent and ability that takes some to the very top and others to middle and lower management careers. To match this fact of life, your beginning recruitment should try to reflect a range of talent and accomplishment, with the majority coming from good middle-level schools, and a few from the colleges that are hard to get into and thus represent a more selective sample of young talent.

The M.B.A. question

This selective screening culminates in the better graduate business schools, where an M.B.A. graduate is a young person who has strong drives for business achievement backed by superior accomplishments that led to admission and graduation. M.B.A.'s are not an unmixed blessing. They are expensive, with starting salaries out of the top business schools well ahead of some of your junior executives, and they sometimes tend to have unrealistic expectations about career progress. And yet when we look at the impressive number of high-achieving CEOs who are M.B.A.'s from the best schools, we cannot ignore the long-range value of these racehorse types who often combine exceptional drives with unusual ability.

Go after the best

Experience has shown that there is a good correlation between school grade achievement and later achievement in business. So it is wise to aim at the top third of the graduating class, if possible combined with achievement in campus activities and sports. Students at an undergraduate business school indicate by that fact an interest in a business career. And yet it is well to broaden recruitment to include liberal arts and science students who show an interest in business. The technical training they get at the business school is less important than the quality of their minds and personalities.

Use your best recruiters

Consistent with your marketing approach, you will want to give yourself the advantage of using your best possible salesmen. It is no reflection on the company's personnel staff to recognize that when a college senior is being interviewed by someone three or four years older who has come up the ladder in your company, he is looking at a powerful persuader, a sample of what he could expect. So by all means program your young hotshots to do their stint of interviewing at the recruiting season.

Use the big guns

At important schools there is nothing as impressive to the candidates as meeting one of the big bosses, so this can be time well spent for your top management. Some companies plan a reception at which the president invites members of the senior class for refreshments and a company presentation.

The college placement officer

It pays to cultivate this important individual who can and does exert quite an influence on who interviews whom and how the students feel about various companies. He can tell you a great deal about current hiring rates and what students are interested in.

Competitive compensation

Again, money talks, and it is unreasonable to expect that your charm and superior salesmanship will bag one of the most interviewed kids for less money than he is being offered by others. Also important in this connection are salary ranges of other graduates who have been with the company.

A visit to the company headquarters

When you have decided that you want someone, it is a good investment to invite him to visit the company headquarters. This kind of trip is exciting to the candidate and gives him an opportunity to size up the company atmosphere as well as the community he may be moving to. Here again, the interview should be carefully planned and the candidate should meet the top people. A few minutes out of a busy schedule are well worth the chance of shaking hands with a possible future top team member for the company.

When you lose one

As in any marketing effort, you can't win them all. But when you had your heart set on an especially exciting candidate and he decides to go with someone else, don't let that be the end of the story. Your personnel chief should keep a file of good ones that got away, and set it up so that in two years' time you get in touch with your lost candidate and take his temperature. Frequently the first job does not work out as hoped and disillusionment has set in. He will be flattered to learn that you remember him, and the trip to your office may result in your hitting the right ball on the second bounce.

17

Rethink
Your Organization
Structure

Form follows function.

—Mies van der Rohe

ORGANIZATION IS A SERVANT,
NOT A MASTER

What, after all, is a business organization? It is a group of
people who work together in an *organized* way to achieve common objectives. True, there have been examples of family
businesses and partnerships where the "principals" operate as
ministers without portfolio, each getting into all phases of the
business. In a large company this would work about as well as
the Tower of Babel in the Bible. And it has long ago been sup-
planted by a philosophy inherent in the Industrial Revolution
itself: division of labor, with responsibility for running the various parts of the business divided up among the top members
of the team. How this is done can have an important bearing

on results, and when we look at companies in need of a turn-around we often find that the organization setup is hurting, not helping, results.

Given the need for coming up with the most productive division of labor among team members, how do we go about it? In sports the team organization is set by the rules. But in business it is influenced by common experience as to what works best, some stimulation from professional students of management, and trial and error. Here are twelve suggestions:

Identify the main functions

Fundamentally, for most enterprises, there are at least five main functions:

1. Creating/designing the product or service
2. Making it
3. Marketing it
4. Financing the activity and controlling it through numbers
5. Acquiring the people to do all this

While obviously functions differ from business to business, the above five elements translate into the following five main functions that will fit a wide range of enterprises:

— Engineering, merchandising, product development, research and development
— Manufacturing, operations, branch management
— Marketing, sales promotion, selling
— Finance, control, planning, acquisitions, EDP
— Personnel, management building, training, labor relations

Pyramid heads

These main functions are normally the basis of pyramid heads reporting to a top management executive, it being un-

derstood that in a small business they may be combined, and
in large ones divided. Moreover, in a large company the top
corporate management is usually made up of the functional
pyramid heads reaching horizontally throughout the entire
corporation plus operating pyramid heads reaching vertically
through geographical locations and subsidiary companies.

Tailored to objectives

When we get beyond the main functional outlines of business organization, the assignment of manpower to any box on
the organization chart should *serve the company's objectives.*
The company invests in people to get results. If it is losing its
share-of-market because its product lines are being outdistanced by competitors, then it needs to build up its merchandising or research staffs. If it is bedeviled by quality complaints, it may have to devote more staff to engineering and
testing. If the bills are not going out on time, the control department may need to be strengthened, and so on.

Sensitive to competition

In all these considerations, the turnaround company must
be sensitive to where the competition is hurting it, and these
areas become prime candidates for strengthening in the organization setup.

A moving picture

The organization chart should not be cast in bronze, because as conditions change the organization setup should reflect them. As the word *organization* itself implies, the change
ought to be organic, that is, related to the living facts of how
the business should operate, rather than arbitrary or precon-
ceived notions. For example, a company that decides that its

most attractive growth potential is through mergers and acquisitions might set up a separate pyramid head for that function.

Tailored to people

The organization setup should be built around people
strengths, and this is another example of the organic development of the team. The front-running performer is interested
in personal growth, and it is wiser to provide this growth for
him and the company by broadening his responsibility than to
run the risk of fencing him in to a theoretically correct organization setup. There is nothing wrong with the unorthodox organization structure that motivates people and promotes top
performance.

Fight empire building

While a desire for personal growth based on performance
is most valuable, a CEO must be sensitive to when this gets out
of line and "vaulting ambition o'erleaps itself." This becomes
empire building when, as in the government, importance begins to relate to the number of people on one's payroll, instead
of how much can be accomplished with how few people.

Divide and multiply

As an antidote to the foregoing, one of the most battle-
tested success principles is to build growth through increased
concentration. Suppose regional manager X has for some time
been way out in front in share-of-market growth compared to
the other regions. Increase his compensation and, if possible,
his title, but sell him on the philosophy that for the good of the
company's total growth his region must be divided into two
and that if he concentrates on a smaller territory with his

usual success he will be in line for a bigger job. Divide and multiply.

Clarity

It is essential that the reporting lines you set up are clearly defined and that they are real, not theoretical. All too often, when you ask someone in middle or lower management "To whom do you report?" you get a smile that implies "Forget the organization chart; I have bosses all over the place."

Job descriptions

To promote this kind of clarity, every job must have a clearly stated job description. Too many managers feel that this is unnecessary red tape because everyone knows what his job is. Unfortunately, in today's complex world, we cannot afford *management by assumption* and the great waste of energy caused by people not clearly understanding their jobs.

Spread too thin

Beware of the temptation to have too many people reporting to one supervisor. This not infrequently creeps into organization structures, sometimes because the strong manager is ready to take on more and more responsibility, sometimes in the hope of saving expense, or perhaps through unawareness of what is wrong with the idea. Even the best of managers, when they have too many people directly looking to them for the help a good supervisor can provide, cannot physically give the time to their people that they need and deserve. As a result, communication suffers, monitoring is weakened, stimulation and training are too infrequent, and the subordinate winds up feeling out in left field. What is the point at which a well-managed group becomes an abandoned crowd? That depends on the nature of the people and the jobs, but as a rule of thumb, especially in top level management, when you get above eight people reporting to you, beware.

Value of manpower planning

As part of the planning function of the business, a three- to five-year plan of executive manpower needs is a tremendous help in keeping your organization structure sound and healthy. (See chapter 16.)

18

Managing
the Team

*When two men in business always agree, one of
them is unnecessary.*

—William Wrigley

Human beings are endowed with certain physical and
mental powers. Each of us can be measured as to these powers:
how fast we can run a mile, how much weight we can lift, what
our intelligence quotient is. Such measurements can establish
the range between the best and the worst in a given group of
people as to these inherent physical and mental powers.

PERFORMANCE VARIES
MORE THAN ABILITY

The fascinating thing is that when we look at the *range* of
individual *ability* as best it can be measured in a group of people, whatever the range is (suppose the best is twice the worst),

the range of the group's *actual performance* will be much wider (the best will be three or four times the worst). For example, the productivity of Americans in industry is falling behind that of the Japanese and some Europeans while our physical and mental fitness is not.

Why is this? It is because human performance is so strongly affected by factors other than physical and mental powers, namely, the emotional and psychological interplay that occurs in group activity. The way people *feel* on the job can make them perform like cripples or champions. The famous Hawthorne effect, which years ago established that emotional factors control rank-and-file productivity, is even more significant in managerial ranks. So when you look at the team you have assembled, you should realize that however good the individual members may be, in the test of action the team will be a winner or a loser depending on how well it functions *as a team.*

BUILDING TEAMWORK

How do we define good teamwork? You have it *when the group performs better than the sum of its parts,* when the team members are stimulated by interaction to make better decisions and achieve higher performance than each could alone.

A team is a group that exists for a clearly stated purpose. It may be a continuing purpose, like a department or a standing committee, or it may have a specific mission like a task force or special committee. Or it may simply be a meeting called for a special purpose.

Tuning up the team

Especially in a turnaround situation where the problems are deep-seated and the company is after a breakthrough into unaccustomed high performance, you need the best in teamwork to get the best in performance from your people.

Here are some of the characteristics of good teamwork:

1. *The group has a clearly stated purpose,* which can take the form of a job description.
2. *The members of the group understand its purpose* and are focused on it whenever they work together.
3. As a result, *the group is doing what it is supposed to do.* It is making decisions, coming up with answers, and, in general, performing participatively to get better results than each member could alone.

Guidelines for building superior teamwork

Superior teamwork doesn't just happen, it needs to be created through skillful management. And while good managements work hard on solving problems, the importance of building optimal teamwork does not usually receive top attention.

Here again there is much help to be gotten from the behavioral sciences, especially by applying Dimensional Management Training or its equivalent.

1. *Leadership is an essential ingredient.* Even where the team consists of a peer group, a chairman should be appointed. Where the members are in different management layers, the leadership will normally come from the senior member, although it is often more appropriate to give the lead to the member of the group who is most professionally competent in the matter under discussion. In any case, the responsibility of the leader of the team is all-important: to see that the group is functioning participatively and is doing its job well. He should be alert to all of the pitfalls and problems of group activity and promptly move in to correct any that surface.

2. *Watch your Qs.* The management must be aware of the behavioral characteristics of the team members and try to set the stage for Q4 or open participative collaboration. If the team is dominated by a Q1 leader or too many Q1 members, decisions will tend to be dictated and members' opinions will at best only be tolerated, and ignored in the final imposed de-

cision. If there is too much Q2 leadership or predominance they are apt to take a minimal view of the scope of their assignment, show little daring or creativity, and try to produce the answers they think are wanted. The Q3 team will not dig deep into their field, will have too many and too long meetings trying to come up with unanimous votes on all questions, with a resultant low likelihood of discharging its mission well. Only in a Q4 team environment can you release the power of cross-stimulation in the group by encouraging candor and a constructively probing approach on all questions, by accepting dissent as a valuable part of the process and by leading the group openly and participatively but firmly toward the prompt achievement of its goals.

3. *Size*. For proper team functioning, the group should obviously be of a size that is big enough to get the benefit of varying shades of opinion but small enough to interact efficiently.

4. *Meeting technique*. The amount of time wasted in meetings in American business is appalling. Even well-organized and effective people will participate in meetings that are routine, boring, and ineffectual, until they come to accept this as a way of business life. Good meeting technique begins with a solid respect for the participants' time and a recognition that a meeting is not a debating society but a *purposeful* activity with a goal to be achieved. Therefore, the subject and purpose of the meeting should be clearly defined and the notice sent out together with all pertinent written material well enough in advance to give everyone the time needed to study it. The participants are then expected to come to the meeting having done their homework and prepared to discuss the questions and express opinions, not to be presented with new material that they have not had a chance to digest and can only discuss off the top of their heads. The notice should also state the approximate duration of the meeting so people can plan the rest of their day, and in the case of regular meetings the dates should be set for a whole year. And if the meeting is chaired in a Q4 manner, open discussion and dissenting opinions will be encouraged, but not rambling and wandering from the subject.

5. *Task-force strategy*. The task force appointed to dig into a special problem is a productive device, especially on matters where there is divergence of attitude in the company. Appointments to the task force should reflect the different shades of opinion, and the members should be able to command the kind of credibility and respect that will sell their final recommendation to the organization as a whole, substituting consensus for divisiveness.

6. *Self-appraisal*. A most effective device for tuning up the quality of teamwork is to have the team members periodically do an appraisal, on a scale of 10, of the degree to which the team is functioning participatively and effectively in respect to: leadership, freedom of speech, dissenting opinions, decision making, pursuit of goals, meeting techniques, etc. Good teamwork not only achieves assigned goals but it also is a powerful training device for developing executive skills in its members. It deserves top management attention and the application of major time and effort.

7. *Line vs. staff*. One of the special benefits of good teamwork is helping to make line and staff people work well together and thus bridge the chasm that sometimes exists between the corporate office and operating divisons.

8. *Tandem top management*. In large companies, given the complexities and technicalities of modern competitive business enterprises, it has often proved helpful to spread top management responsibility beyond the chief executive officer. Most commonly this results in a tandem top management, with a chairman and a president, one as chief executive officer and the other as chief operating officer. For this to work ideally, the two should have complementary strengths. If one is a marketer, the other might have a background in production or finance. Sometimes the tandem becomes a troika, with a vice-chairman rounding out the picture. These concepts work well or don't work at all, depending on the personalities and behavioral characteristics of the individuals, but they can be very effective and play a positive role in building the total management team.

PART IV

The Power of Bifocal Planning (The Road Map)

Perfection of means and confusion of goals seem to characterize our age.

—Albert Einstein

19

Principles of
Planning

A pint of sweat can save a gallon of blood.
—General George S. Patton

THE LESSONS OF PLANNING

One of the most powerful lessons to be learned in the world of action in our time is that however well equipped we may be for a course of action the end result will be closely tied to the skill and thoroughness of planning that went before. Shooting from the hip may have its excitement, but not for the investor. Especially in our times, as the rate of change keeps accelerating, thorough planning before action is neglected at our peril. And so throughout the world today, high-achievement business management puts great emphasis on what is here termed *bifocal planning,* with professionally developed short-term and long-term plans, a prerequisite to desired performance.

103

UNDERLYING PRINCIPLES

Here are ten *underlying principles* involved in successful planning:

Eliminating surprise

If you are driving a high-powered vehicle over tricky terrain, you want to know what lies ahead. No matter how good your reaction time and agility may be, you don't want to have to cope with the unexpected at high speed. Therefore, one of the main purposes in the life of the professional manager is eliminating surprise and traveling a charted course with the lights on. The planning function is management's way of anticipating the forces that will affect future performance and then developing programs for achieving desired results in the expected environment. The plan becomes the launching pad for successful action.

Planning breeds confidence

Another important source of the power of planning is the confidence it inspires in those who are expected to achieve it. When George Bernard Shaw said, "You can make any of these cowards brave by simply putting an idea into his head" he was dramatizing the power that suggestion has over confused and aimless people, a power that has been amply illustrated by hypnotic leaders throughout history. Especially in a turn-around situation, with its mood of discouragement and concern, the people yearn for a plan they can believe in, because it brings the hope of a solution to their problems.

What is your business?

The health and future of your company is often vitally affected by the way you define the business you are in. In our lifetime we have seen the railroads change from the most gilt-edged investments to harrassed survivors of a different past, partly because their managements believed they were in the railroad business instead of the transportation business. In their quest for profitable growth, well-managed companies have usually found that their best bet is in diversification that fits within a broad definition of their business, rather than in completely unrelated fields.

CEO Involvement

Planning does not come naturally to people. By inclination many will work hard on day-by-day tasks but be "too busy" to get involved in planning. Their private view is apt to be that planning takes up a lot of time, after which you wind up doing what you would have done without it. This short-sighted approach is often the way of the underachieving company, which is left behind in its industry by the front-runners whose managements are busy planning where they want to be in the near and distant future.

To correct this and bring in professional planning as a way of life requires committed leadership by the CEO. He needs to communicate to his executive team that the company is embarking on a new planning process that will become a major force in improving performance, and that he expects full support and participation throughout the company in making it work. More than anyone else in the company, the CEO should be mentally living in the future, pondering the opportunities and threats in the company's path, and continually shaping the picture of the company five or ten years down the road.

Keep planning simple

With the growth of planning as a subject of interest at business schools and management associations, writings on the subject have become more and more complicated and technical. Reading and hearing about these the businessman is easily put off by the mathematical formulas, grids, and charts. He is apt to feel that the whole planning bit is academic, lighter than air, and far removed from the core of the business. As a protection against this, here are three suggestions:

1. Keep your written planning work simple, editing out abstruse or academic material not readily understandable by your team.
2. Strive for precision in your data and avoid too many generalities.
3. Make sure that the heavy emphasis is on the few key factors that make the big difference in the company's performance. To scatter your shot over too many targets will mean more misses than hits.

Insight into markets

One of the most important ingredients in successful planning is a deep understanding of your customers and the big and little changes going on in your markets. This calls for research, awareness, a study of trends, and instinct.

Anticipate competition

As part of the planning process, management should, from close watching of its competitors, try to figure out what *their* plans are most likely to be. More and more managements nowadays are articulating future plans in their stockholders' reports and in appearances before financial analysts. All this should be factored into the future shape of your markets and your position in them.

Build a sense of urgency

A well-developed planning environment will help to destroy complacency in an underachieving company and replace it with a growing feeling of impatience with things as they are. As your people get used to thinking of their performance in relation to plan, it will speed up the reaction to change and develop an individual and group will to achieve—the first requirement in a turnaround.

Plan versus last year

Because stockholders and financial analysts look at performance in comparison with last year's, too many companies have their major attention fixed on *last year* in reports and discussions, rather than on *plan*. This often becomes one of the diseases of the ailing company, what we have called driving with your eye on the rear-view mirror. If the plan is well done, the lessons of the past have been learned and are reflected in the plan, and the planned figures become the most accurate picture of expected levels of performance and thus a more valid basis for monitoring results than comparison with last year. Management's attention then moves forward from postmortems to making the desired future come true.

Underpromise, overachieve

Most turnarounds at first require a major shift toward a more conservative level of planning. What we are after is to develop a new habit of beating plan in place of the old one of usually missing plan. In the problem company, the management's deep embarrassment with its results keeps it from planning ahead on a realistic level in line with what the company has been doing. The only way out of this dilemma is to face the facts and devote plenty of careful thought in each sector of the company to finding a planning level that is not too easy but can still be realistically achievable. Then the turnaround company can begin to have the necessary experience of beating plan and acquiring self-confidence as a springboard to steady improvement in planning and performance.

20

Winning over
the Team

Skill and confidence are an unconquered army.
—George Herbert

Let us for a moment take stock of where you are now on your way to a turnaround. You have your new management team in place, some brought in from the outside, some inside promotions. You have good reason to think that this new team will give the company an improved level of skills that can be put to work to take the company toward its objectives.

ADDING CONFIDENCE TO THE SKILLS

Now what is needed to put these new abilities into high gear for getting results is to create a good level of confidence throughout the organization, a shared belief in the management's mission and a growing conviction that the frustrations of the past are on the way out and a new period of success is on the way in.

A MILESTONE COMMUNICATION

In a turnaround situation, as in life in general, you can't always wait until everything is in place before you act. Logically, it might be sound to delay talking to the whole organization until you have done the long- and short-range planning and completed the strategies. But this would rob you of a valuable opportunity to reap the benefits of a morale surge as you start on the long and difficult road to a turnaround.

Your people all know that the company has not been doing well for a long time, and even if the unpleasant facts have not been emphasized, they leave an undercurrent of unhappiness and concern. When important management changes occur, rumors start flying and hopes are aroused. At a time like this, then, the whole organization is anxious to hear about what is going on, and eager to change its mood to one of enthusiasm and confidence.

What is called for is a companywide executive meeting, lasting most of a day, to answer the prevailing questions and leave the whole organization with a strong and positive picture of the new thrust in the company. This is highly beneficial when done well, producing a dramatic surge in morale and often an immediate improvement in business. Such is the power of emotions over human performance.

What the CEO says to his assembled executive body on this occasion is in the nature of a milestone and deserves the most careful preparation. Here are nine suggestions:

Setting the tone

You, as the CEO, should, from the beginning, typify the maxim "Underpromise, overachieve." Deal with the company's past clearly, briefly, and gracefully, without belaboring bygone mistakes. You are undertaking a long and difficult job, so reflect confidence without bragging, and stay away from your past accomplishments at other companies. Your people will not fail to hear about these, but at this meeting they are sizing you up and are eager to find out about your character and how good a leader you will be.

Introduce the top team

Explain that the purpose of this meeting is to introduce the top team and tell the whole organization about the company's new direction. As mentioned before, it is best to stay away from the word *turnaround* and instead talk about improvement and building the fortunes of the company. The danger in applying a turnaround label is that it may raise false expectations of instant remedies and a fast cure. When, as is bound to be the case, the hard-won improvements involve time and some disappointments, bold talk about turnarounds breeds cynicism and shakes confidence. A turnaround is what others will talk about after it is accomplished, as a result of management's having worked consistently and professionally for the company's improvement.

Dual program

To achieve a turnaround means curing a company's deep-seated shortcomings through careful planning and skillful execution, which, in time, will soundly reposition the company for the future. But without compromising this essential long-range building program, management must, at the same time, do everything possible to improve current results and gain the growing support of the team. Depending on the gravity of the problems, this may mean anything from an immediate improvement in earnings to a slowing up of the profit slide, or even merely a curtailment in the growth of losses. In any case, the company's management needs to understand that there will be a dual effort going on simultaneously, seeking improved current performance while planting the seeds for the company's repositioning.

Defining the business

It should be made clear that what is said at this meeting is preliminary to the thorough job of planning and strategy development that will follow in the months ahead. Nevertheless, it is important for the new top management to give the organization its preliminary picture of how it defines the company's business and its mission.

Competitive position

This is followed by management's description of the markets being served, the strengths and weaknesses of the competition in each market, and where the company stands in the competitive lineup. Out of this would naturally follow an indication of where the major opportunities lie for the company's growth, as well as the obstacles threatening that growth.

The planning process

Explain the results-getting power of the comprehensive planning process being launched. Enunciate the principles underlying professional planning outlined in chapter 9, especially the importance of regularly achieving and beating plan, moving the focus from last year to this year's plan, and the proven benefits of this approach in gradually and permanently raising performance levels. And tell the team that to support the dual program mentioned before, the planning will be bifocal, namely a current short-range plan tied into a strategic long-range plan. Finally, it should be emphasized that everyone present will be involved in a planning process that works from the top down and from the bottom up, so that the plans finally adopted will represent the combined thinking and judgment of the whole group, supported by strong conviction that the plans will be achieved.

Strategies

As part of this comprehensive planning process, strategies will be developed for shaping product mix, marketing effectiveness, operating productivity, optimum deployment of company assets, financing expansion, and so on.

Participative management

It will be helpful at this point to tell the group what the new top management has in mind as its philosophy of running the company, namely participative management under leadership that wants the whole group's free and spirited participation. To foster this working environment a most important tool will be Management by Objectives (MBO), a proven device for effectively eliminating confusion and frustration and helping people to achieve and surpass desired results. Management information systems will be designed to serve these objectives by providing the most helpful information tools.

New standards

Finally, the group should be left with the idea that the company is embarking on a period of gradually rising standards in all phases of the business. The new standards will be arrived at carefully and participatively and will help to take the company up the ladder in its industry to where it belongs. Whether the CEO can be more or less specific on this subject will depend on the circumstances.

21

Improving
Current
Performance

Never give up and never give in.
                              —Hubert Humphrey

Managing a turnaround is like living in a house while it is being renovated. While on all sides work is underway to improve the building, you must manage to carry on effectively during the process.

COMMITMENT TO TIMETABLE

Because the remedies needed in a turnaround usually involve conditions that have existed for years, all concerned must recognize that a successful and durable turnaround takes time—usually three to five years. Therefore, this time frame needs serious commitment on the part of the management and the board of directors. In the meantime, in order to keep

113

that support, it is very important for management to do two
things:

1. *Eliminate unpleasant surprises.* If there is no way of
avoiding some further deterioration in earnings, this must be
projected conservatively so that the actual performance, if it is
on a down trend, will still be better than management said it
would be.

2. Make a strenuous effort to *find ways of improving current earnings,* without compromising the long-range turnaround program. Experience has shown that when strong new
leadership comes into a situation, there can be a companywide
boost in morale, which can produce a burst of energy that
brings improved results. In addition, the special skills of the
new leadership can be expected to be productive in the short-
range as well as the long.

CURRENT IMPROVEMENT PROGRAM

Here are twelve suggested steps for achieving current performance improvement while work on the long-range turnaround is in progress.

Get everyone into the act

There can be a gold mine of bottled-up improvement suggestions in people's minds throughout the organization. To get
at this, the head of the business should take the time to have
one-on-one meetings with department heads, aimed at establishing relaxed and candid communication and surfacing correctible problems. If you can hold these meetings in the department manager's office instead of your own, it will go a
long way toward breaking the ice on relations with the boss, as
well as getting him to open up. Take careful notes, and make
it a point to let people know what happens on the suggestions
they have made. Without this follow-through the reaction will
be that suggestions may be listened to, but they are not taken
seriously.

Employee suggestion program

A companywide suggestion program is another way to flush out productive ideas from the rank and file and, as a by-product, to build morale and confidence in the new leadership. A committee screens the suggestions and sends explanatory replies on those not used. Rewards are given for suggestions accepted, with suitable fanfare and top management involvement.

Spend money to make money

Let it be known in all departments that the company is willing and eager to invest in new equipment and methods provided a return on that investment can be demonstrated. If there has been a lack of participation in the past, you can expect a number of big and little suggestions, many of them usable.

Clarify objectives

Review the current plans that are in effect, revising any that are clearly unattainable. Then publish the new plan and communicate to all that these are now the realistic objectives that they are expected to achieve.

Eliminate roadblocks

In problem companies cumbersome procedures tend to accumulate, becoming built-in obstacles to achievement. These roadblocks can be flushed out in your meetings with department heads, and they deserve prompt remedial acton. A frequent gripe is the unwieldy approval procedure, where, for example, a salary increase requires approval by the personnel

department plus three or four layers of management, right up
to the CEO. This Maginot Line of expense control hurts
rather than helps the bottom line, because it buys frustration,
loss of good people, and contempt for top management. Modern management works with budgets or plans and holds managers responsible for achieving them, so that approvals are
narrowed down to exceptional cases. The elimination of roadblocks can be one of the most productive measures for improving current performance by freeing up people to work at their
jobs.

Streamline programs

Review worthwhile programs already in effect to see if it is
feasible to simplify their execution and get to the finish line
sooner. At the same time, you may want to postpone or eliminate those programs that are questionable.

Go after sales

Nothing will improve the bottom line quicker than a surge
in sales. Therefore, a strong participative effort aimed at stimulating current sales volume is of the first importance. Communicating with customers and finding out how they view the
company can often lead to pay-off ideas for improving sales.
Review your sales promotion and advertising and come up
with a new look and a fresh promotional approach. Plan a
new sales contest that will capture the imagination and enthusiasm of your sales force. And analyze the service end of the
business for weaknesses that can be strengthened by a drive
toward a new standard of service.

Expense reduction program

This is a far-reaching subject deserving of a lot of attention
and effort. It also requires judgment, monitored by top man-

agement, to see that expense cutting concentrates on the elimination of waste and does not go beyond that to hurt quality of product, service to customers, or the long-range objectives of the company. All too often companies in a profit squeeze get caught in a downward spiral by resorting under pressure to expense reductions that gradually undermine the company's market position.

Your expense program should include these steps:

1. *Compare your expense rates* (percent to sales) by department with other companies in your field. This kind of data may be difficult to obtain, but it deserves consistent effort to accumulate, because nothing is more helpful in shaping up your own operation. Sources of this information include:
   (a) your employees who have come from other companies
   (b) companies comparable to yours that are not competition because they operate in different parts of the country
   (c) interviews of managers from competitive companies for possible openings in yours
   (d) trade associations
2. *Compare head counts* in functional segments of the company with similar counts in prior years. This filters out inflation and focuses attention on the actual forces doing the work.
3. *Zero-based budgeting* may be helpful as an approach, because it starts with the assumption that no expense is justified unless it can be shown to be necessary and justifiable in the amount budgeted. The cost-benefit relationship, the comparison of a cost with an evaluation of the benefit derived therefrom, is a useful exercise at this stage of a turnaround.
4. *Declare war on duplication,* overlapping, unessential activities, and unjustified overtime. Where possible, reduce the frequency of meetings and reports.
5. *Cut fat, not muscle.*

Modernize methods

Out of your meetings with department heads you can expect to develop a list of improvements in operating methods as well as equipment. Along with this go better work measurement and higher standards.

Managing time

Give some thought to what can be done effectively to help your associates with the universal problem of making the best use of their time. Books and courses on the subject are available, and can be translated into a streamlined training effort that should pay off.

Use task forces

With the multitude of things you are trying to get done, the use of task forces with weekly progress meetings is recommended.

Talk bottom line

Focus the attention of all team members on net profit and cash flow, revising reports to reflect these more strongly, if necessary.

22

The Profit Plan—
Short-Range,
Tactical

They can because they think they can.

—Virgil

PLANNING THE ROAD MAP
THAT GETS YOU THERE

You are now ready to tackle the key job of making the planning process a vital ingredient in your turnaround. There is no short cut to the kind of professional planning that high-performance managements do. It takes a lot of time and effort and it is worth it because, unless you trust to luck and hoped-for windfalls, there is no successful substitute for using a road map to get where you want to be.

In bifocal (short-range/long-range, or tactical/strategic) planning, these two sets of plans are worked on at different times of the year.

PLAN VERSUS BUDGET

A word about nomenclature. In the past, most companies referred to their annual plans as budgets, and some still do. If your company is one of these and still works with budgets, you may find it advisable, as part of your turnaround program, to adopt the word *plan*, referring to short-range as well as long-range planning, for the following reasons:

1. This helps to differentiate the future from the past.
2. The word *budget* has a negative image, with disciplinary and restrictive overtones. It is thought of primarily in relation to expense, where it functions in the manner of a housewife's budget, which she tries not to exceed. It also has horrendous overtones of helpless failure as used in government. The planning process, on the other hand, while it has its disciplinary side, goes beyond that to represent a positive picture of where you are going in sales and the components of profit.
3. There is merit in using the same word, *plan*, for both short and long-range planning, since both are part of the same process of establishing a road map for all to follow.

THE PERIOD PLANNED

The duration of the short-range profit plan varies in different companies from one year to three months. What has been found to be most productive is a six-month plan developed in complete detail for the first six months of the fiscal year. Work on the first six-month plan is begun three months before the end of the fiscal year, and it is put to bed during the final month. In order to come up with a projection for the whole year to give to the board of directors, a less-detailed estimate for the second six months is then prepared and added to the detailed first six-months' plan for the year's projection.

Then, in the third month of the new fiscal year, work is begun on the detailed plan for the second six months, to be completed in the fifth month of the fiscal year. In this way, you do your planning close enough to the period to avoid hazardous crystal-balling of distant months, while at the same time giving yourself a six-month plan that normally will cover the lead time of most operating commitments (see Table 1).

TABLE 1. SHORT-RANGE PLANNING SCHEDULE

Months of fiscal year	10	11	12	1	2	3	4	5	6	7	8	9
	Next year's first six months' plan			Estimate second six months for year's projection			Second six months' plan					

PROFIT PLAN COMPONENTS

A halfway plan will not do the job. The plan must include all of the profit components from sales and revenues down to the bottom line of pretax and after-tax profit. Otherwise you are driving with part of the windshield covered.

These are the items normally planned in a six-month profit plan:

Dollar sales
Percent better or worse than last year
Gross margin dollars (sales minus cost of goods sold)
Gross margin percent to sales

In retail and wholesale businesses it is usual to plan the components of gross margin as well: *initial markup, markdowns,* and *inventory shortage, all in dollars and percent to sales.* In other businesses this breakdown is also useful if it applies.

Dollar expense
Percent expense to sales

The expense components should follow the main functional responsibilities of the organization, all in dollars and percent to sales. For each profit center the profit plan is broken down in more detail than the corporate plan. Where the profit center might have ten or fifteen expense categories in its profit plan summarizing voluminous operating reports, the corporate profit plan often limits itself to two categories, direct expense and corporate expense.

Where applicable, *other income* (nonoperating) and *other expense* are included. Many companies also show a separate line for *interest expense*, reflecting the critical importance of this item in recent years.

Dollar pretax profit
Percent pretax profit to sales
Cash flow

BOTTOM-LINE PLANNING

There is a rather important point that needs to be made in connection with profit planning. Many companies limit the responsibility of those in charge of profit centers to those items in the profit chain that they can functionally control. For example, payroll is considered directly controllable, rent and taxes not controllable. As a result, this kind of plan arrives at a bottom-line figure called *contribution*, representing the profit before all other "uncontrollable" Items. Here is why *contribution planning is detrimental* compared to real bottom-line or pretax net planning:

1. In underachieving companies we frequently find that profit center managers think they are making money for the company when they are not, because the figures they look at are sugar-coated, since they leave out part of the grim reality of the so-called uncontrollable ex-

pense. This *creates an atmosphere of false euphoria* and weakens the profit drive in the company.

2. *Is it true that expenses are either "controllable" or "uncontrollable"?* Often the word *uncontrollable* means that the expense cannot be controlled in the day-to-day operations of the business. Yet it can be changed by an out-of-the-ordinary course of action. In any event, top management has to cope with all expense no matter how it is labeled, and when it is hit by a jump in "uncontrollable" expense, tries to find a way to make up for it. Moreover, experience has shown that a company does better when profit burdens and motivations are shared as broadly as possible and not limited to the front office.

3. *Bottom-line planning is a great training device* for developing managers who can cope with the whole gamut of producing a profit.

PLANNING PROCEDURE

These are suggested steps in developing the short-range, or tactical, profit plan:

1. In a turnaround situation, begin by reviewing the existing plans and laying bare the reasons why the company has not been achieving them. The determination must be to break the destructive chain of unachieved plans by adopting a firm policy of conservative planning that will be achieved and exceeded. Throughout the process, top management must *root out wishful, optimistic planning* not supported by the facts.

2. As in all planning, *the process should be top down and bottom up*, meaning that first the general signals are established by top management, next the detailed planning is done by each profit center, and finally the profit center plans are reviewed by top management, which, after renegotiating any unacceptable portions of the

profit center plans, combines them into a total company plan.

3. The *general signals* referred to include conclusions as to the economic outlook as it affects the industry, and the level of total company sales for the planned period. This is based on a review of sales trends in recent months, on a comparable basis with last year, eliminating any new operations added since last year. In the planning process recent trends should be given more weight than past trends. For example, if for the last full year the company was 7 percent ahead of the previous year, but each of the immediately preceding three months ran + 5 percent, + 3 percent, and + 1 percent, it would not be prudent to plan the next six months at + 7 percent. Factors influencing the company's performance should, of course, be given consideration in tempering the recent sales trend. But especially in a turnaround situation it is important for the first new thrust not to result in more missed plans. Therefore, management must resolve to produce a realistic conservative plan that, given all the known facts and expectations, is likely to be exceeded in the performance.

4. This overall company sales profile is then reflected in *each profit center's planning*, depending on how that profit center did in relation to the total company in the past year and in recent months. For the planning activity to bring improved results, it is essential that each profit center manager work in the same frame of mind as top management, and understand that he will be held responsible for delivering results that are better than the plan.

5. In *putting the component plans together* into a total company plan, top management frequently finds that the bottom line is shockingly disappointing. This can be a critical moment in a turnaround. If the CEO, feeling that the plan is unacceptable and not good enough to be taken to the board of directors, sends it back to the operating managers and *orders them* to improve

the plan, then his turnaround program is derailed. Why? Because his people will feel that nothing has changed, that the new plan is plastic rather than real and cannot be achieved. Dealing with this dilemma requires very careful analysis of the plans of the profit centers, and interaction with their managers to seek areas of potential improvement that are realistically attainable and not based on unfounded optimism.

6. Another way out of this dilemma is "two-level" planning, covered in the next chapter.

23

Two-Level
Planning

Wisdom liketh not chance.

—Old English Proverb

A CORPORATE DISEASE

We have seen how destructive it is to any hopes of a turn-around for a company continually to miss achieving its plans. It is a dangerous corporate disease, which, like alcohol to the alcoholic, destroys individual credibility and establishes a loser mentality that becomes extremely hard to dislodge. The company that suffers from this disease has a defeatist state of mind and a listless, aimless company environment. As for the planning process, it is derailed.

THE DILEMMA

When the moment arrives for an underachieving company seeking a turnaround to put together a profit plan, it often has to face the following dilemma: The attempt to arrive at a realistic, conservative plan that the company can probably achieve usually results in a planned performance level that is not very good and will not in itself herald a turnaround. The first reaction of a turnaround manager to such a plan may be "Gee, if I can't do better than that, I won't be much of a hero." This is a moment of danger, because if he succumbs to this fear and arbitrarily hypes the plan to make it look better, he is exposing his whole turnaround program to a miscarriage at the start by not breaking out of the plan-missing, loser habit. The real dilemma, therefore, amounts to this: Which is better at this early stage of a turnaround, a disappointing plan or a disappointing later performance? Turnaround history has shown over and over again that it is better to face up to a realistic plan, make sure everybody recognizes that it is conservative, and then go on to give your organization the thrill of overachieving.

PRUDENT TIMING

A two-level planning process is obviously more complicated than the single plan, and not all turnaround managers will want to undertake it at the outset. Considering the capacity of the organization to absorb change, it may be more prudent to go along for a year with a single plan and introduce two-level planning as a second phase, after the company has demonstrated its ability to achieve plan performance and gradually tune up results.

THE VALUE OF A SECOND
LEVEL OF PLANNING

The advantage of two-level planning as practiced by many successful companies is that it provides a sensible way of assuring that performance will run above plan, and at the same time gives the team the stimulus of a more flexible *objective*, or *goal*, which is still within the range of possible achievement.

In this way, while doing the necessary to assure accomplishment of the plan, you provide a level above it to accommodate growing performance.

DEFINITIONS OF THE TWO LEVELS

In working with two-level planning, it is important to see to it that the definitions of the two levels are made clear to all concerned:

Plan

Plan is best defined as the result that, given the situation expected to prevail during the period of planning, will have a high probability of being achieved. It is a conservative level, not far from the worst that can realistically happen. In fact, it is sometimes called the disaster plan, meaning that if the economy turns down or unfavorable conditions develop in your operating environment, you still expect to achieve the plan. It should be understood by all that the plan is put at that level because from now on beating the plan will be a must in the organization and that barely achieving this plan is just an *adequate* performance, a 3 or 4 on a scale of 10.

This last point is one that you may not be ready for at first, because you may feel it better to assign a higher rating to achieving plan in the first period or two, in contrast with the history of missing plan. But as performance responds to turnaround efforts, before long the plan should regularly be beaten by a considerable margin. At that point the evaluation of barely making plan should settle into its proper niche of merely adequate, or a 3 or 4. And it should be understood that merely adequate performance in an achieving organization does not bring promotion or, ultimately, job security.

Objective or goal

The *objective* level, which some companies refer to as the goal, starts out with a sales level reflecting an increase over last year of *2 to 5 percent above the plan figure.* The other profit components vary from the plan only to the extent that these additional sales make possible. Thus gross margin, depending on the nature of the business, may be expected to show some improvement in percent to sales (perhaps 0.1 to 0.4 percent) in response to increased sales and less need for cutting prices to clear out inventory. In the expense category, the dollars should be increased over the plan figures only to the extent that the additional sales require expense dollars to service them. The percentage of expense to sales should therefore come down. As a result, the profit dollars and percent to sales should both be higher, and the same should be true of cash flow.

In appraising performance in a high-achievement company, getting results at the objective level is deemed to be doing what one is paid to do and therefore rated "good" or a 5 or 6 on a scale of 10. Performance at 2 to 4 percent increase in sales *over* the objective level, with corresponding results in the other profit components, would be rated "very good," a 7 or 8, and anything above that "excellent," a 9 or 10 (see Table 2). Remember, these ratings are geared to high performance, and in the early stages of a turnaround it may be advisable to use more generous ratings as a temporary morale builder.

FLOW-THROUGH

A highly effective technique for stimulating profit performance as part of the planning process, and which is not used widely enough, involves highlighting the percent of the additional sales dollars over plan that flows through to pretax profit (see chapter 40).

THREE-LEVEL PLANNING

As an interesting variant on what has been presented above, one highly successful company uses a three-level planning process, as follows:

1. The plan, expected to be achieved and surpassed.

TABLE 2. SUGGESTED PERFORMANCE RATING SCALE

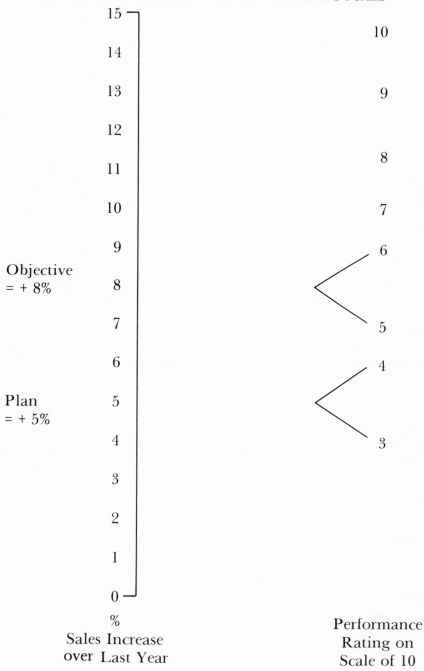

Objective
= + 8%

Plan
= + 5%

%
Sales Increase
over Last Year

Performance
Rating on
Scale of 10

2. Planned results if sales are 10 percent less than plan. The managers think through in advance all the measures that would be taken to safeguard the planned pretax profit in the event of a 10 percent shortfall in sales.

3. What the numbers would be if sales are 20 percent less than plan, again incorporating a strong effort to anticipate all the protective steps that can be taken to safeguard the planned profit under extreme difficulties.

This kind of planning is an example of how the planning process can play an important part in producing results—in the case of the company in question an unbroken record of stellar profit growth for many years. It would not necessarily fit all businesses, and requires a high degree of management skill to be effective.

24

Flexing the Plan

You have to adjust your running style when you're running on ice.

—William Proxmire

PLANNING AS A PROFIT TECHNIQUE

Short-range, or tactical, planning, as described in the last two chapters, is a technique for helping a company's profits by:

1. Laying out the near-term course of the business that has a high likelihood of being achieved and surpassed, based on
   (a) the recent trend of performance
   (b) adjustment for known and expected changes in marketing and expense factors.
2. Monitoring performance against the plan and taking necessary result-getting action.

RESULT-GETTING ACTION

For the manager who works this way, the plan guides him in what to do to improve his business. As he watches his daily and weekly reports, he looks for areas of the business that are falling short of plan. Suppose a certain department has been running 10 percent behind plan for a number of weeks. If the plan was properly done, it took into account all the known factors and was put at a conservative level that all agreed should be exceeded. The shortfall signals the department's manager to find what is causing the problem by digging into all phases of the operation and getting the input of those involved. This makes it possible to take corrective steps early. Similarly, his supervisor and management up the line gain an early awareness of performance lags against the agreed-upon plan, and begin asking questions and stimulating constructive action.

These are the everyday components of running a business dynamically, and the better the planning process the more timely and accurate will be management's moves. This is the proven way to escape from the shackles and hindrances of an ailing business where management action is defeated by unrealistic plans, from a defeating bewilderment in approaching problems, and from the many other enemies of a turnaround described in chapter 6.

LAST YEAR VERSUS PLAN

Why is it better to compare current performance with the planned figures instead of last year's? If nothing ever changed, last year would be just as good. But under shifting conditions, a manager who probes performance shortfall against last year with his people will be up against an endless barrage of excuses based on things that have changed since last year: the calendar, the customers, prices, and so on. All this alibiing slows down action, and leaves middle managers feeling the boss is unreasonable, and the boss depressed by an inability to get things done.

COPING WITH THE CHANGING SCENE

Working with the plan instead of last year's figures should greatly reduce this kind of static, because the plan has already taken into account known changes since last year. But how do you cope with changes that have occurred since the plan was made? Here we face two concerns:

1. Planning involves a lot of work. You do not want to load an unreasonable amount of additional man-hours onto the operating people who make up the plan.
2. Changing the plan could lead to confusion as to what exactly is the yardstick against which performance is measured, with a resultant weakening of the plan in the eyes of the organization.

THE TECHNIQUE OF FLEXING

Professional planning recognizes the need for sensitivity to events through working adjustments to the plan as the period progresses. The key words are *working adjustments*. The figures in the plan remain the official plan and yardstick against which performance is appraised during the period. What has been added is a tuning mechanism, the better to control the flow of current investment into the operations of the business.

For example, the plan envisioned a certain volume of monthly sales, supported by an appropriate buildup of inventory through manufacturing and purchases, as well as the dollars of expense needed to make those sales possible.

Now, let us say sales in department A are running 50 percent ahead of plan and in department B 40 percent below plan. Assuming these trends have been in evidence long enough to be a valid indication of what is likely to continue, then if we stay with the inventory and expense figures in the plan, what do we face? In department A a coming out-of-stock condition, disappointed customers, and a missed opportunity for sales and profit growth. Department B, on the contrary, will have its bottom line wrecked by serious overstocks and ruinous expense.

Of course, the speed with which we can build up A's inventory and reduce B's inventory and expense will vary from business to business. But the earlier we recognize such conditions the sooner we can get them corrected, whatever the prevailing time frame.

Flexing, then, is a practical way of controlling the flow of inventory and expense in response to changes up and down from what was envisioned in the plan. The flexing process should be handled by the control division, because it is not necessary to burden the operating people with this figure work. The control division makes flexing changes in inventory based on guidelines. It is not workable or necessary to change expense figures correspondingly, because operating people should be watching expense as a percent of sales and following the principle that when sales are below plan try to keep the plan percent to sales, when sales are above plan try to hold the dollars of expense increased only by expense needed to support the additional volume.

YARDSTICKS FOR FLEXING

1. It is a fact in most businesses that both inventory and expense can be increased much faster than they can be decreased. An overstock frequently takes months plus downward price adjustments to get back into balance with slowed sales. Expense cutting is seldom immediately effective. In recognition of this state of affairs, some companies *flex more conservatively on the upside than on the downside.* For example, they would adjust the inventory and sales plan for only half the current *increase* over plan, but for 100 percent of any *decrease* below plan.

2. To *avoid too many insignificant changes*, it is suggested that no change be made unless sales for a given department or division are running at least 20 percent up or down from the

plan during the recent past, for whatever length of time is considered enough to establish the trend as meaningful. A usual period would be two or three months, and this should screen out the insignificant shorter ups and downs.

Reverting to our example, suppose department A was planned at 10 percent over last year for the six months' planning period, with the figures broken down appropriately by month. We now find that for the past three months sales of this department have been running 60 percent ahead of last year instead of 10 percent, and there is reason to expect this trend to continue for the balance of the period. The procedure in this case would be to put half of the 50 percent increment over plan into the next figures, that is, to plan the remaining months of the period 10 percent plus 25 percent for a new figure of 35 percent over last year. The control department would then issue adjusted inventory and sales plans for department A factoring in a 35 percent increase for the remaining months. Using only half of the increment over plan (25 percent instead of the actual 50 percent) is a prudent protection against the possibility of overstocks, should the 50 percent drop to 40 percent or 30 percent in the next months. And experience has shown that it is wise to expect a faster turnover of department A's inventory under these conditions.

In the case of department B, which was also planned at a 10 percent increase, the recent trend is 30 percent behind last year, 40 percent below plan. In this case the inventory and sales plans should be adjusted the full minus 40 percent in the interests of eliminating unsupported optimism, which must lead to profit problems.

Anyone who watches economic statistics knows how critical inventory levels are in the health of the economy. Flexing is a useful device for fine-tuning a company's inventory control and keeping it from getting out of balance with sales trends.

25

Long-Range, or Strategic, Plan

If you don't know where you're going, any road will take you there.

—Theodore Levitt

THE POWER OF STRATEGIC PLANNING

The development of the long-range strategic plan for a business enterprise can be exciting, stimulating, and productive—or it can be a big bore. It all depends on the quality of the effort: how well it is done, who are involved, and how it is used.

There is no doubt that a company with a first-rate strategic plan built into the fabric of its business thereby improves its chances of attaining superior growth in sales and earnings over a period of years. It costs time and money to do effective long-range planning, but the return on such an investment can be great. Especially in a turnaround situation, strategic planning is essential.

137

WHAT IT WILL DO FOR YOU

There are four main reasons why companies that plan well do better:

1. The strategic plan *clarifies the nature of the business,* what it aspires to be, and where it is going. It dissipates the fog of drift, opportunism, and management by crisis, replacing it with purposeful management by objective.
2. It *builds morale* in the organization and the will to achieve, which is the precondition of success, most of all in a turnaround.
3. It *channels action* throughout the company to where it will be most effective in getting the desired results.
4. It *accelerates achievement.* Experience has shown that the long-range plan kindles in good managers a strong desire to achieve in year two what the plan called for in year three or four.

BENCHMARKS OF STRATEGIC PLANNING

This chapter presents a general introduction and procedural outline for a company approaching the development of a long-range strategic plan. Obviously, it cannot cover the smaller details nor attempt to tailor procedures to any particular kind of business. Here are some of the the key principles that make for success in strategic planning:

1. Take *enough time* to do the job right. Any attempt to squeeze the long-range planning process into strip-model proportions will undermine the quality of the plan, and the lesser amount of time used is apt to be wasted.

2. *Broad involvement of people.* A strategic plan developed by outside experts, or even by top management alone, might make an interesting document, but it will not produce the kind of results to be had from a thorough participative effort throughout the organization.

3. Strategic planning needs to emphasize *open-end, conceptual thinking* so that the plan is enriched by creativeness and imagination from many sources in the organization. Without this input the plan is in danger of being merely a pedestrian laundry list of dos and don'ts without the insights that release new energies and new directions.

4. Because of the time and wide involvement necessary, it is advisable to begin with a detailed *timetable and assignment list* for the planning process itself. The process should be two directional, *from the top down, and from the bottom up.* This means that the planning process moves from top management, or corporate office, to middle management, or operating executives, who perform their functions and submit the results back to top management, who then put the plans together, critique them, and may resubmit parts of them to middle management for additional work before finalizing the complete corporate plan. The size of the company will affect the logistics, but not the process itself.

We are now ready to deal with the development of a strategic long-range plan, step by step. The planning period is usually five years, and while there may be situations where a longer term is advisable, the five-year plan fits our turnaround situation nicely. Moreover, we are talking about a rolling five-year period, with plan updated each year and taken one year further.

Here is a suggested procedure for developing a five-year strategic plan.

ELEVEN PLANNING STEPS

1. Identify participants

In order to get orderly involvement at different levels of the business, committees are recommended, as follows:

Central planning committee, made up of the chief executive officer, the chief operating officer, and the pyramid heads reporting to them for marketing, production, accounting and control, and administration-finance.

Divisional planning committees. A planning committee chairman is appointed in each important division of the business. The chairman then selects the individuals (not exceeding a workable number) who will collaborate on planning assignments. The chairmen of divisional planning committees may be pyramid heads serving on the central committee. If they are not, the divisional chairman should serve on the central planning committee, where feasible.

2. Environmental forecast

The central comittee is responsible for setting the stage to the best of its ability (using outside help if necessary) for the conditions under which the company will be operating in the next five years, including economic, demographic, and competitive factors, such as:

National economic trends in GNP, employment, inflation, appropriate income and expenditure statistics, all for the last five-year period and the next five-year period.
Forecast changes in demographics affecting your industry.
Trends affecting your competitive environment in the last five years, and expected changes in the next five years.

This environmental background information is given to the divisional committees as a jumping-off point for their work, but they are free to question and suggest changes in any part of the environmental assumptions based on their close-up observation of their own situations.

3. Mission statement

The central committee is responsible for preparing a statement of the company's mission, that is, the nature of its business, the guiding principles under which it operates, its long-term objectives, and a description of the skills needed to achieve these objectives, including:

    leadership skills
    marketing skills
    planning and goal-setting skills
    production-engineering skills
    expense and asset management skills

The mission statement should be much more than a pious generalization. It should be a well-thought-out statement from various levels of the organization about what you want for your customers, what you want to market, what you want the customers to think of you, and how you will be differentiating yourself from your competition. The mission statement should also include major financial objectives and uses for capital to achieve the objectives of growth in market share, productivity, return on investment, and cash flow.

Finally, the mission statement should include the company's responsibilities to its constituencies: employees, customers, vendors, shareholders, and the communities in which it operates.

Here again, to make the mission statement a productive force in the business, it must be developed participatively, the first draft coming from the central committee, additions and modifications from the divisional committees, and the combined finished statement again coming from the central committee. Most important: A company's mission statement is never finished. As long as the planning process goes on, it is constantly updated, clarified, and shaped toward action.

4. Competitive positioning

Here is where the planning process appraises your performance against your leading competitors during the past five years by business segment as well as in total, and identifies trends in your competitive positioning in the industry. Included are any announced and otherwise known future developments by competitors that will have a bearing on your positioning, as well as changing forms of competition, expansion, market segmentation, and company size.

This is one area of planning in which information may not be readily available, and yet it is obviously of great significance to any company planning its future to gather data in as much detail as possible about the other players in the league. As in the other planning components discussed above, the competitive positioning information is prepared by the central committee and fed to the divisional committees, who are expected to add their input, with corrections and amplifications, for later review by the central committee.

5. Main business plan

This is the most detailed part of the strategic plan, because it covers the business you are in. Using all the information developed so far, the central committee does a first-draft projection of total company sales, profit components, pretax earnings, percent return on sales, capital expenditures, total investment, and return on equity for the last five and the next five years. It may also include figures showing the impact on pretax net profit (flow-through) of each additional 1 percent of sales increase over last year.

This is where the divisional planning committees begin to function. They schedule meetings to review the central committee's total company data on environmental forecast, mission statement, and competitive positioning, and come up with their assessment of their division's performance and standing compared to the total company. The assessment should be descriptive as well as in numbers. This preliminary discussion on environment, mission, and competitive positioning requires time and is most effective in an unstructured environment outside the office. It should be an exciting introduction for your operating people to the heart issues of the company's and their future. It is important for the chairman of each divisional committee to create an atmosphere in which people are not afraid to open up, suggest wild ideas, or participate in free discussion and brainstorming.

The next step for the divisional planning committee is to go through each segment of its business and list strengths, weaknesses, opportunities, and threats. The strengths and weaknesses are identified as those that already exist or are inherent in the division as it is. The opportunities refer to new achievements made accessible by using those strengths and correcting the existing weaknesses. The threats are the identification of possible developments outside the division that would be harmful to its fortunes.

The division then uses this inventory of strengths, weaknesses, opportunities, and threats to influence its projection of the course of business for each department or segment of the division over the next five years, and ultimately produces and forwards to the cental committee its business plan, corresponding to the central committee's total company plan.

6. Programs to implement the plan

Along with its business plan, the division prepares and forwards to the central committee copies of its programs for achieving the main results in the plan.

7. Internal expansion

The central committee establishes the return-on-investment requirements (hurdle test) for new capital expenditures, and makes it clear to the organization that the company is looking for and encourages capital expenditures that meet the test through the various avenues of sales expansion, higher margins, or expense savings. The divisional planning committee follows through on its appraisal of strengths, weaknesses, opportunities and threats, to come up with suggested capital expenditures for internal expansion, and prepares acceptable return-on-investment projections to be submitted to the central planning committee.

8. Total company main business plan

The central planning committee is now in a position to review and assess the quality of the individual planning efforts by the divisions, consideration being given to the written programs for achieving identified opportunities sent in by the divisions. It is to be expected, regardless of how much advance briefing is done, that where many participate in a strategic planning effort, there will be variations in judgment and point of view. This is a fact the central planning committee has to identify and deal with.

So that normally there will be some divisional plans sent back with comments questioning the degree of optimism or pessimism, and aimed at achieving a more uniform approach by all the divisions, rather than dictating to any of them. Through this top down, bottom up process of interaction, the central committee arrives at the point where the component divisional plans are ready to be combined into a total company plan.

This combined company plan is then compared with the first draft originally sent out by the central committee, and the committee talks out any material discrepancies, giving more weight to the combined plan, which has the benefit of the input of the entire organization.

9. New avenues of expansion

The central committee now reviews and revises the mission statement and considers the advisability of entering into new kinds of business compatible with the mission statement. While this is a vital and all-important part of strategic planning for a company that is doing well, it would not normally be among the first priorities of a company in a turnaround situation. Expansion into new fields involves more than average risks, and therefore such a venture should be fortified by demonstrated management strength and track record. Expanding weakness is a sure ticket to disaster.

In considering compatible new businesses, a company must clearly evaluate the market for the new products, the competitive situation, the availability of necessary manufacturing and marketing skills, and arrive at a pro forma profit projection that meets the hurdle test of required return on investment.

10. Mergers, acquisitions, and asset redeployment

The next step is for the central planning committee to talk out, based on the projections for the next five years by the divisions, whether any consideration should be given to asset redeployment by divestiture of parts of the company. A segment of the business that has been a severe drag on profits for some time and shows little hope of improvement over the next five years, even assuming that management problems are solved, raises the question of whether the assets involved could not be put to more profitable use by the company. In a turnaround situation this is frequently the case, and often is among the first steps taken by a new turnaround management.

Similarly, possibilities of merging the company into a larger and more successful one cannot be overlooked, although in a turnaround situation it usually makes more sense for the new management to try to achieve a turnaround before considering a merger, since the company would be worth much more after a successful turnaround, if indeed it still were interested in that possibility.

The advisability of seeking to acquire another company would depend on many factors, beginning with your company's financial situation. It is true that a good many turnarounds have involved diversifying the business through astute acquisitions, but this is not a surefire remedy or easy game. It has been most successful where a well-financed old-line company with lack-luster recent earnings has shrewd and dynamic top management and acquires well-managed companies with good prospects.

11. Financial plan

We now have all the ingredients to assemble the company's strategic plan. At this point it is advisable to do a financial plan projecting balance sheets for the next five years. From these are determined the *capital needs* to implement the strategic plan, and the resultant picture is tested against the financial policy in the mission statement.

As a guide to financial decision making it is well to treat the financial plan as a model on three different assumptions:

> *Pessimistic* — little expansion, sales 10 percent below strategic plan.
> *Moderate* — strategic plan level.
> *Optimistic* — rapid expansion, sales 10 percent over strategic plan.

In addition, cash flow should be projected for each of the five years under these three different assumptions, as this will influence the capital needs.

INTEGRATE LONG- AND SHORT-RANGE PLANS INTO BIFOCAL PLANNING

The completed strategic five-year plan, accepted by the whole organization that has had a part in fashioning it, will be little more than a waste of time and effort if it is not put to work to get results for the company.

First, it must be made clear to all concerned that the strategic plan numbers are all at the *objective* level, not at the ultraconservative plan level referred to in chapter 23.

Next, the figures in the strategic plan should be compared with current-year objectives througout the company, to make sure that when the first year of the strategic five-year period begins everyone's objectives will tie into the strategic plan. A good time to do strategic planning is a relatively slow middle part of the year. In that case the strategic plan figures will be available before the objectives for the next year are written.

At the same time next year and in subsequent years, the strategic plan is reviewed by the same committees and extended for another year, as well as adjusted for any material changes in conditions.

IMPLEMENTATION

To implement the strategic long-range development of the company, this follow-through is needed:

1. Update the manpower plan, reflecting the personnel needs to support the implementation programs in the strategic plan.
2. The planning process itself may have disclosed or highlighted weaknesses in division teams that need to be dealt with.
3. Study the options available for financing the capital requirements in the strategic plan, and decide on timing and action.

BEWARE OF THE HOCKEY STICK

Throughout the process of long-range planning, we should recognize the human tendency to be optimistic about the future, the farther ahead the more optimistic. We often find that managers, in planning the next five years, will be rather conservative for the first two, about which they are best informed and nearest to being held accountable. When they get to the last three years the skies brighten and optimism leaps into the saddle. On a graph the resultant projection looks like a hockey stick, with the first two years relatively flat and the next three turning up at a sharp angle to form the handle. Don't accept hockey stick plans unless they are defended by convincing documentation.

PART V

Turnaround Strategies (The Motor)

The highest task of intelligence is to grasp and recognize genuine opportunity.
—John Dewey

26

Trend
Marketing

The voice of the people is the voice of God.
　　　　　　　　　　　—Alcuin (Epistle to Charlemagne)

MARKETING BEGINS WITH
AWARENESS

Winning strategies, the motive power that moves companies into high achievement, are rarely Einsteinian feats of
imagination and discovery. In real life successful strategic decisions are born of deep awareness of the forces affecting a
business, molded by intuition and judgment. A company that
goes through the process of developing a first-rate strategic
long-range plan has come most of the way toward fashioning
its major winning strategies.

In any industry there are a variety of strategies being applied by different companies. There also may be some that run
their business without identifying any particular strategy or
strategies.

For a turnaround company, as for any company that wants to do well, the first step is to realize that battles and wars are not won without battle plans or strategies, and that the same applies to competing companies.

In Part V we describe some of the principal winning strategies in evidence among successful companies.

IMPROVING SALES

The most pressing need in a turnaround situation is sales improvement. There is just no way to achieve consistent earnings growth over a period of years without a meaningful improvement in the sales curve.

why

The most basic strategy for turning the sales curve upward in a company is tied to the magic question: *Why should the customer buy from me?* (see chapter 9). To insure that there are positive answers to this question throughout your product lines, three things are needed:

1. *Keen sensitivity to how the customers feel*, whether positively or negatively, about each product that you sell.
2. *Recognition that customers' feelings and judgments are volatile* and constantly changing, and that this fact of life is further stimulated by competitive product changes and innovations.
3. Your ability to *see your own products objectively* and not defensively.

These marketing truths apply most forcefully in retailing, where volatility and change are at their highest, but their lessons are valid in any business operating with customers in a free market economy.

TREND MARKETING

Trend marketing recognizes that any marketed product, like any living organism, has a life span, and that during this life span, its vitality first rises and then falls (Table 3).

In Table 3, the horizontal line relates to how long the trend lasts. The vertical line measures the strength of the trend in terms of total sales.

TABLE 3. CURVE OF CUSTOMER PREFERENCE

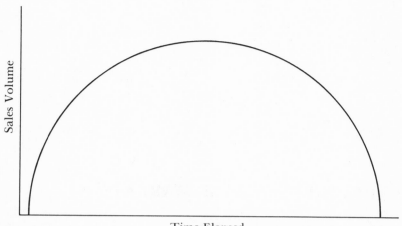

The shape of the curve, of course, varies from product to product. Some products that become fads have a brief life of high intensity, like the hula hoop (Table 4). Others, like white bedsheets, have had a life span going back for centuries, only to decline in our times because of the introduction of color and design (Table 5).

TABLE 4. THE HULA HOOP

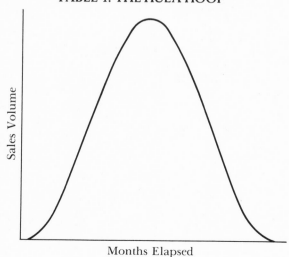

TABLE 5. WHITE BEDSHEETS

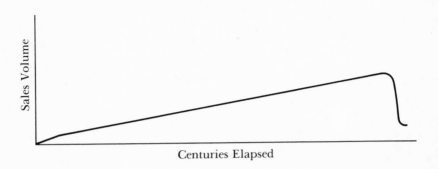

FIVE STAGES OF TREND MARKETING

In working with the trend marketing concept, it has been helpful to recognize five stages in the trend curve (Table 6): testing, incoming, prepeak, postpeak, outgoing, defined as follows:

TABLE 6. TREND MARKETING

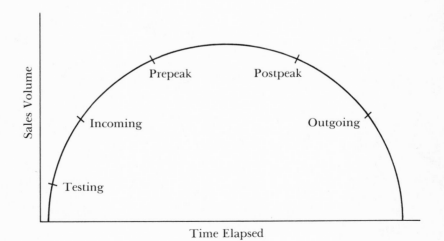

Testing

A new product of uncertain demand that is being presented to customers in a limited way so as to test its marketability. Companies that frequently test new products are often leaders in their field.

Incoming

Testing having been favorable, the product is enjoying growing demand, often with low availability. A company marketing a product deemed to be in the incoming stage faces an important and difficult decision. The product is still in its infancy and the questions are *how big* is the potential demand, and *how long* is it apt to last. The decision involves risk and capital investment keyed to building sales and capturing share-of-market.

How does one answer such a question? If you are trying to predict the future full-grown size and longevity of a child, you would look at the family history in relation to what you observe about the child. Much the same process is used in making product forecasts: the relationship of this product to others already in the field, the pace of its growth and acceptance up to now, and research into customer preferences.

Prepeak

When a product reaches this stage on the trend curve it is still growing in sales, but the *rate of growth* has flattened out or begun to decline. Business is still very good, sales are climbing and this is the period of optimum profitability, with demand running high and supply having hit its stride.

Postpeak

At this stage of the curve the product is still selling well with good profitability, but now sales *(as well as rate of growth)* have flattened out and begun to decline. Here management needs a forecast of how gradual or precipitous the sales decline will be or whether the decline is temporary and sales will start up again to a new peak. Staying with a product that is postpeak, still selling actively and profitably, is apt to be tempting, but management needs to decide how much longer to remain committed to the postpeak item. These decisions are complicated and affected by investment factors, but the point being made here is the importance of awareness that the product is at the postpeak stage on the trend curve and that this must be properly taken into account in the company's marketing plans and decisions.

Outgoing

At this point there is no longer any doubt that the product is on the way out. Its sales are dropping everywhere, although some customers may still be asking for it. The farsighted management will have phased this product out by now, or at least tapered it off to the point where it is not a profit drain. Companies that get caught with heavy commitments to outgoing products face painful losses in the thankless job of trying to liquidate inventories of unwanted goods.

MAKE TREND MARKETING
WORK FOR YOU

Trend marketing is a strategy for getting your customers into the decision-making process in your business. It is not simple to apply, but cultivating it assiduously will pay off handsomely. Six factors are needed:

Skill in testing

Developing effective testing procedures is a must. This will vary according to the business you are in, but study what other companies do to test-market products similar to yours and develop your own program for pilot testing your products in ways that produce valid and reliable input as to potential demand.

Information flow

Regardless of how computerized your reports may be, you must have timely and regular information on the sales of each product, including percentage better or worse than plan and last year, share-of-market percent (try to get this), and percent to the total category in which the product belongs. In a modern computer setup, you can have it programmed to show whether the *rate* of sales increase for a product is rising or falling, to help early recognition of products that may be moving into a postpeak phase.

Talk-outs

To help you get the feel of trend movements in the market, there is nothing better than regular meetings of those closest to the picture to air their opinions on what is happening with the trend curve of a given product. These talk-outs should include those involved in selling, designing, and advertising the product. They should be supplemented with feedback from your customers, sought on a regular basis. If these talk-outs become a regular part of the marketing process, it will not only enable you to identify where each product currently fits on the trend curve, but will also raise companywide consciousness of the importance of watching customer preference trends.

Company trend profile

Following through with this approach you can arrive at a total company trend marketing profile. By adding up the marketing commitments involved in all the products identi-

fied as testing, incoming, prepeak, postpeak and outgoing,
you can arrive at a picture of what percent of your total marketing effort is in each of these categories. Clearly, there is no
one ideal profile for all companies, but as illustrations, case
one below looks healthy and case two looks sick.

CASE ONE		CASE TWO	
Trend Category	% of Marketing Effort	Trend Category	% of Marketing Effort
Testing	5%	Testing	2%
Incoming	15%	Incoming	8%
Prepeak	45%	Prepeak	20%
Postpeak	25%	Postpeak	30%
Outgoing	10%	Outgoing	40%

Blend trend strategy with long-range plan

You can now take a fresh look at your long-range strategic
plan in the light of your conclusions about the company's current marketing trend profile. Out of this can be developed a
program for strengthening your trend rightness, as well as a
five-year trend road map that can be incorporated into your
long-range strategic plan.

Risk taking

Successful marketing involves risks. Playing it safe is just
too dangerous, because too often it means being left at the
post unresponsive to the changing customer. Timidity, fear of
change, turn a company to the past instead of the future,
clinging to declining markets and barred from growth areas,
until *the company itself becomes outgoing*. Which tells us that
companies, too, can be identified by where they belong on the
trend curve!

27

Segment Marketing

I feel like a fugitive from the law of averages.
—Bill Mauldin

DIVIDE AND MULTIPLY

The lessons of the exceptional marketers of our generation have been powerful, and for the most part they add up to the dictum "divide and multiply," that is, grow, amoebalike, by dividing yourself into more and more identified growing parts.

The wisdom in those words applies widely in business but nowhere is it more valid than in marketing to today's consumers. If you offer your products indiscriminately to all potential customers, you will be outdistanced by the competitor who, having analyzed the whole range of customers, zeroes in on those groups or customer segments that share the same characteristics. With his rifle approach he is bound to hit more

159

targets more accurately and effectively than anyone can with the shotgun approach.

THE RIFLE OR THE SHOTGUN

When Miller High Life decided that if it wanted to close the gap between Miller and industry leader Anheuser-Busch it would have to do somehing more than just sell beer, it moved into a segment marketing strategy. Miller decided there was a part of the total beer market that was calorie-conscious and developed a new low-calorie light beer with an advertising approach tailored to this segment of the market. This strategy was so successful that Miller almost succeeded in catching its competitor, which soon adopted a similar strategy. Thus we see the power of segment marketing at work in the beer business.

Market segmentation has been a growing strategy throughout consumer industries, and it is being applied successfully in other fields. So that today, companies without a segmented approach to marketing may be vulnerable. The American automobile industry, for example, which has for years practiced segment marketing in developing its many car models, was late in accurately defining the needs of major segments of their market for lighter cars with low fuel consumption, and the penalty for this oversight has been enormous.

IDENTIFYING MARKET SEGMENTS

Any marketing work must, of course, be tailored to the needs and conditions of your company. To identify the market segments best for you, analyze the total market for your industry's products and find those segments with the most potential for what you can produce. This becomes the basis for developing your segmented marketing program.

By way of illustrating what is meant by market segments, here are ten customer profiles representing segments of today's consumer market.

Children

Buying decisions theoretically made by parents, but strongly under the influence of the children who, in turn, are under the influence of television and other children, with strong peer-group conformance. In the next decade this segment will be a declining percentage of the total population.

Students

Also projected to be a declining percentage of the total, also strongly influenced by television and conformity, this group has significantly changed in its outlook and values since the sixties and early seventies.

Young Marrieds

As the now grown-up postwar baby boom, the 25- to 44-year-old group will be the fastest growing during the next decade or so. These young homemakers are price-sensitive, careful, label-reading shoppers who seek quality within their budgets and occasionally save up for something fine as an investment.

Working Women

Now more than half of our female population, they have emerged as a big new target in consumer marketing. This customer has sophistication, knows her own mind, does not spend a great deal of time shopping, is interested in quality.

Singles

This growing group is less homogeneous, since it includes people of either sex living alone as well as paired households of either or both sexes. Price-conscious buyers, less interested in quality or permanence, with strong peer conformance and firm preferences.

Blue-collar workers

More emphasis on price than quality, less sophisticated taste, receptive to macho appeal.

Aspiring young executives

Urge to emulate those who have arrived where they want to go. As buyers, they know what they want, shop widely, look for bargains.

Affluent conservatives

Interested in service, top quality, not price-sensitive, have cosmopolitan tastes.

Empty nesters

These are the families whose children have moved out, as well as retirees and senior citizens. This is one of the groups expected to grow as a component of the total population. Careful buyers, avoiding unnecessary purchases, price-sensitive, desirous of service.

Ethnic groups

Of growing importance, especially regionally, wide variance in tastes and preferences, requiring a specialized marketing approach.

These segments are, of course, not mutually exclusive and any one customer may belong to several groups. In the main, however, each segment has its own characteristics.

CONSUMER RESEARCH

A management attempting to find its way through the maze of customer types in our melting-pot society needs the help of professionalism in the form of consumer research techniques. These range from employing market research consultants to using in-house specialists able to mount marketing surveys, interview customers, work with customer groups, and so on. The important thing is not so much to arrive at a catalogue of people profiles as to develop a clear picture of the mental and social characteristics of each group, as a basis for shaping your product and promoting it to its segment of the market.

IMPORTANCE OF DESIGN

With the growing sophistication and taste of the American public, product design, the visual aspect of the product, has become an increasingly powerful influence in the sale of a product. It is hard to think of anything today, from garbage cans to telephones, where the quality of the design itself does not make a big difference in the product's success. It should therefore be an important concern of any marketing program to see to it that the product design and packaging can stand up to competition, or be ahead of it.

It should be emphasized that while the examples in this chapter necessarily deal with the consumer field where the segmenting approach to marketing has flourished, the same principles can bring results in other fields, even including heavy industries. In the end every customer is a person.

28

Shaping the Product Mix

Every disease is a physician.

—Irish proverb

Trend marketing and market segmentation go a long way toward putting and keeping a company's product lines in tune with its best market opportunities. The next marketing strategy follows logically from the previous two and goes on to *shape the product components* (mix) of the business for optimum sales and profit results.

MIX STRATEGY

It may seem obvious that, just as an individual ought to follow healthful living habits and stay away from harmful foods and activities, a company should mold its business so as to emphasize products with a healthy demand and good bottom line, shunning those that are harmful to earnings. But the sad fact is that business aberrations from the logical and healthful course are, if anything, more prevalent than those of the individual.

There is no single strategy that has paid off more handsomely to businesses all over the industry spectrum than a strong and continuous *mix strategy*.

The *objectives* of such a strategy are as follows:

1. *To build profit through mix.* With the same sales, a better mix will produce a better profit.
2. *To build market share and dominance through mix.* The better the mix of a business, the more it appeals to its market and the more its customers are disposed to buy.
3. In a turnaround situation, *to provide a ready demonstration of profit improvement potential*, raising confidence and morale while spreading profit consciousness within the company.

HOW TO IMPLEMENT AN EFFECTIVE MIX STRATEGY

Because of the somewhat obvious wisdom of shaping a company's product mix, this strategy, like many self-evident truths, is often taken for granted and winds up with little more than lip service and feeble follow-through. The following ten steps will help you to fashion a mix strategy that, judging from widespread results achieved in industry nowadays, offers sure and prompt help in a turnaround situation:

Identify product group

Think of your company as a collection of businesses, each one a product group made up of similar characteristics: market target, manufacturing and cost structure, marketing approach, and inherent profitability. Group your products into a workable number of such groups, perhaps a dozen or so.

Return on investment by group

Recognize that each of your company's product groups, considered as a business, represents a flow of investment that needs to be justified by a satisfactory return on that investment. Underachieving businesses sometimes cling to product lines through habit or tradition. Pride in a company's history and its past glories is the enemy of change and turns off the exercise of open-minded judgment. This can leave the company fighting a hopeless battle against *today's* competition with *yesterday's* products. In arriving at the return on investment (ROI) of a product group, consider not only the actual present return but the *potential* return. If the product group has certain quality defects that can be remedied, or if the marketing effort has been inadequate and can be made effective, then you need to estimate what the ROI would be when these corrections are in place. Also, in looking at individual products in a group you cannot always apply rigid ROI standards, because certain products may be necessary to round out the group assortment or establish a quality range, and therefore deserve to be in the product group in spite of their ROI.

Effect on total company ROI

Taking the company's ROI standard as determined in the long-range strategic plan, the product group ROIs should make it possible, with the proper mix, to arrive at the company's ROI standard. If, after analyzing the product group ROIs, this does not seem feasible, then to turn around the company it will be necessary to look beyond the present lineup of products for the profitable employment of the company's assets. This, of course, ties into the long-range strategic planning effort described in chapter 25 and to the trend marketing and segmented marketing strategies covered in the last two chapters.

Market strength and profitability

In each product group study its customer acceptance, share of the market, and competitive posture. In most cases a product group that produces a good return on sales and investment is also one with good customer acceptance and market strength. If the product stands out in its field, the customers prefer it, buy it readily, and your pricing is relatively free from competitive profit-margin pressure. Conversely, there are product groups where distinctiveness cannot be attained, so that your company is offering the same thing as your competitors, prices are footballed, and there is no discernible way to make a profit.

Evaluate potential

At this point you are in a position to line up the product groups in terms of their desirability and what their contribution might be toward setting the company on the road to consistent profitable growth. This should be done by the central strategic planning committee, either as part of the long-range planning effort or as a separate development of a mix plan.

Three- to five-year plan

Decide which product groups you want to grow and which to deemphasize or drop. Develop a three- to five-year plan of what top management considers feasible in growing the desirable product groups, and express this in dollars and percent of sales to total company sales. Also develop similar product group figures expressing those that will be deemphasized or dropped over the next three to five years. Bear in mind that a company in a turnaround situation must proceed with caution in dropping *any* business without replacing it with additional

sales elsewhere. Otherwise it may be exposing itself to a further profit squeeze by the effect on expense ratios of too many
drops in sales. A good principle in this case is to plan to *hold
the sales dollars of deemphasized product groups at their
present level* without either increasing or decreasing. As the
growth areas expand, the deemphasized groups become a
lower percentage of company sales and a smaller part of its
product mix.

Projection of results

For each product group produce a pro forma operating
statement showing sales and profit components down to pretax net, expressed in dollars and as a percent of sales and ROI.
Make operating projections for each of the years planned, and
then combine them into a total company operating statement
showing the expected results of the proposed mix strategy.

Gain full support for the mix program

The next step is to sell the mix program to the organization
with an appropriate presentation by top management. Obviously those in charge of product groups targeted for growth
will be enthused, and the others apprehensive. It is therefore
important to explain to the managers of the negative groups
that their individual careers will not be hurt by the mix strategy for two reasons:

1. Performance will be measured against objectives re-
    flecting the expected results of the mix program, and
    those who achieve and surpass these objectives, es-
    pecially in bottom-line performance, will achieve full
    recognition.
2. Plentiful individual growth opportunities will be open-
    ing up in the course of the company's development, and
    these will be available to all good performers.

Implementation

With top management backing, the operating divisions then develop detailed programs for growing the desirable product groups. These may involve additional investment in equipment, space, sales force, advertising, design, and so on.

Monitoring results

To make all this happen, what is now needed is a new set of weekly or monthly reports showing sales and profit results by product group, so that the results of the programs may be closely monitored. These reports should feature the percent of each group to the total company, since that expresses its portion of the mix and how it is doing against the long-range plan.

SHAPING MIX FOR A TURNAROUND

A hard-hitting and effective mix program is a tremendous asset to a business. As with many of the building blocks of a turnaround, it can only be achieved through a good deal of concerted and participative effort on the part of the management team, constant spotlighting of progress or lack of it, and tuning up and revising the growth programs as needs are revealed.

29

Selling and Sales Promotion Strategies

The finest eloquence is that which gets things done.

—David Lloyd George

TIRED-BLOOD SELLING

In a turnaround situation, a company's selling effort often suffers from tired blood. A history of not achieving plans and quotas and losing share-of-market is bound to pull down self-confidence and morale in the selling organization. In self-defense, the sales team shifts the blame to other divisions of the business, such as product design and manufacturing, the general attitude being "If we had the right products to sell, we could do as well as anybody."

Given the urgent need for sales improvement in a turnaround, one of top management's first concerns must be to get the selling troops into a winning streak. This takes time, of course, but it is often amazing how soon improvements can be obtained by changing prevailing states of mind from negative to positive. It is difficult to motivate the customer when you are not motivated yourself.

PROGRAM FOR STRENGTHENING THE SELLING FUNCTION

A well-rounded program for strengthening the selling function of a business includes the following:

Leadership

In business, as in baseball, you don't win pennants by accident. It takes management that excels in team building. The first step is to get yourself the right kind of leadership for the selling arm of the business, which may mean recruiting a new general sales manager from within or outside of the organization (see chapter 10). If you have to go outside, beware of the failed big-time sales manager. You will generally do much better with the younger man on the way up who is burning for the opportunity to head a sales organization and make his mark.

Appraising the team

The next step is to take the measure of each member of your present selling team (see chapter 11). Remember that what you are after is *potential*, and you have to distinguish between the incompetent who is miscast and the low performer who could do better under the right leadership. In a turnaround situation it is wise first to do as much as you can with the people you have, under better leadership. Except for the clearly incompetent, avoid too many changes at the outset. Bloodletting is an outmoded medical treatment.

Incentives

It will help motivate the sales force if new incentives are introduced into the compensation method. Since whatever was in effect before did not work well, nothing will get the sales force's attention quicker than a new set of commissions or bonuses tied to objectives. The management should be sensitive to the annual levels of salesmen's compensation *compared to competition*, since it is difficult to attract and keep good producers if your team is underpaid. Three kinds of incentives can be considered:

1. *Commissions or bonuses on total sales*, sometimes graduated to heighten the incentive at different levels.
2. *Special bonuses* encouraging the sales of the more desirable product lines, as part of a mix strategy.
3. Periodic *contests* designed to generate a burst of enthusiasm and improve results during a specified period. In a turnaround situation there is no better way to change the mood of a dispirited sales force and galvanize the team into action than with a well-designed contest featuring exciting prizes. You can pick up ideas for effective contests by following the sales management press, observing what other companies are doing, or getting outside help from specialists.

Training program

Underproducing members of a sales team can be new recruits who are floundering or old hands who have become bored. A first-class training program will do wonders in instructing the novice and revitalizing the drifter. Those companies who may not have the in-house capability to develop a professional sales training program can buy appropriate material on the outside. And this is another area in which behavioral sciences have recently made a contribution to selling effectiveness, by techniques such as the dimensional approach described in chapter 13.

Better selling tools

Take a critical look at your brochures, leaflets, and other selling material, including packaging, compared to those of your competitors. These devices are important parts of the communicative process between your company and your customers, and you are dealing with customers who are exposed to state-of-the-art advertising skills in magazines and on television. So if your material looks old-hat or out of step with the market, your sales representatives are being put at a disadvantage. Here again, the upgrading of your sales material can be done in-house if you have the available talent, or else by resorting to outside specialists qualified to do everything from redesigning your logo to preparing printed material and advertising.

Action reports

One of the essential ingredients in a winning sales operation is a regular flow of the right kind of performance reports to each member of the team, letting him know how he is doing and keeping him motivated. There are three kinds of reporting problems that can be turned into opportunities:

1. *Timeliness.* Sales performance reports that come out late are like serving cold and shriveled food long after dinnertime to people who have lost their appetite. To the salesman they suggest that the management does not care enough about what it is doing to let him know promptly. In a turnaround situation, therefore, the management can make a positive impression with the selling team by launching a "hot-off-the-press" sales report.

2. *Comparability.* Sales reports usually show this year's performance against last year's. But things are always changing—realignment of territories, loss or shifting of accounts, different timing on promotions—so that the salesman's head is full of reasons why this year is different from last year, and in fairness to him these should be taken into consideration in judging the performance. With that kind of smoke screen, the drive to achieve is undermined. But a cure is readily available. A carefully developed sales plan that takes into account all the known and expected changes included in this year's program enables management to compare this year's performance against an alibi-free plan figure that the sales team helped to develop.

3. *Clear format.* Too many sales reports are hard to read or require the user to perform calculations to get the full meaning. In addition to actual dollars of sales, here are suggested action-oriented items of proven effectiveness:

Dollars better or worse than plan
Percent better or worse than plan
Cumulative dollars better or worse than plan

This way of showing results highlights precisely how successful or unsuccessful the performance is, and the cumulative version is a constant reminder of where it stands for the period. A salesman who keeps reading how much *worse* he is doing than he said he would will be a lot more motivated than one reading two sets of figures without a pointed comparison.

Shaping territories

Carving up markets for maximum sales effort can be a creative task. A turnaround company will often run with the same territorial assignments for years, with a fair amount of apathy as a result. Perhaps a realignment of territories based on an appraisal of individual sales representatives will generate a fresh approach and new enthusiasm. Moreover, some territories may just not be economical to cover, whereas others may deserve more intensive cultivation.

Accent on service

In looking for ways in which a struggling company can get a leg up on a competition, the area of service beckons. We are living with deteriorating service on all sides with growing buyer resentment as a result. Therefore, going after a noticeable improvement in service and building a service state of mind in its organization is a good strategy for a company in a turnaround. Those companies, in whatever industry, that are really service-oriented generally have a strong and durable hold on their markets.

Advertising

Our generation has seen revolutionary changes in communication techniques that have opened up important new areas in business. In a free-market economy the buyer is influenced by an unending barrage of communication in addition to personal contact with the seller: direct mail, newspapers, magazines, television, movies, and hearsay. So that the competing company's success depends in large measure on the skills it brings to fashioning its advertising program for the most effective use of its advertising dollars. And it is gratifying to note that these skills, in their modern form, have originated and reached their highest development in America, so that American advertising style has been adopted all over the free world. The management of a turnaround company should therefore take a fresh and searching look at all aspects of its advertising program:

Theme. Is there a consistent theme or approach that fits the competitive situation and convincingly appeals to the customers' interests?

Copy. Does the wording of the ads speak with the true voice of the company? Does it, in addition to getting the story across, convey the right overtones about the company? Compare your advertising copy with that of your most successful competitors and judge whether or not your customers might take it to be old-fashioned or boring.

Layout. Is the visual impression and layout of your advertising attention getting and does it make it hard for the customers *not* to read at least the most important messages? How does your layout compare to your best competitors'?

Typography. Does the type face used reflect the company's character and personality? Are too many type faces being used, thus blurring the picture? Are the right sizes of type being used for readability and emphasis? If the total advertising represents the *voice* of the company, the typography is the *tone of voice* and the size of type its *volume.*

Media. Along with the tremendous physical changes in advertising, there have been enormous shifts in its distribution to the various media. Is your advertising reaching your audience efficiently by appearing in those print and electronic media best able to reach it?

Budget. How does the money your company spends for advertising as a percent of sales compare to your more successful competitors? This does not imply that in a turnaround you should immediately expand your advertising budget. It may be more prudent first to improve the effectiveness of your present advertising dollars, and second to channel more of those advertising dollars to those product groups that have been selected for maximizing in your mix strategy as well as in your trend and market segment strategies.

Choosing your advertising agency. Judging advertising skills can be confusing and difficult. Recruiting an ad agency should be approached in the same way as recruiting a company executive. It deserves careful consideration of their past performance for others, their understanding of your business and its competitive problems, samples of past work, and, of course, their presentation of what they have in mind for your company. Once engaged, their work should be monitored and appraised from time to time, just as in the case of your own executives, and if their performance does not achieve its objectives they should before too long become a candidate for replacement.

Customer research. In shaping an advertising strategy that is right for your company, there are some questions that can best be answered by the customers themselves, through professionally done questionnaires and interviews. This valuable research aid need not be very costly, because there are usually simple and direct ways of having a meaningful dialogue with customers through the mail, by telephone, or face to face.

Promotional strategy

Depending on your industry, there is a variable mix of promotional techniques, such as special discounts, rebates and bonuses, and clearance sales.

Ideally, a company with good sound products and market credibility should not have to resort to this kind of sales needling as a major part of its marketing strategy. While it may get you some business at first, it cuts into gross margins and encourages customers to feel that the main reason to buy from you is price, instead of the unique character of your products, quality, and service. Still, there are times when sales need special stimulation, and various industries have established patterns for these promotional efforts. Furthermore, when an industry is in the doldrums during a recession, promotions rise in frequency and intensity, as in the case of the automobile industry in 1981 and 1982.

In a turnaround situation a company is apt to be burdened with more slow-moving inventory than is ideal. Sometimes this inventory has been around for a long time, its presence based more on hope than on fact. Especially at times of high interest rates, but really at any time, a company cannot afford to have its capital tied up in unwanted merchandise. So a high turnaround priority should be to clear out this kind of stock and shift investment into actively selling inventory.

Testing

Throughout the process of updating marketing strategies, it makes sense, when a major change is contemplated, to try it out in a small way as a test. If it does not work you have not been badly hurt. If it does, then it is the time to move into it on a large scale.

30

Production Strategies

Somewhere something incredible is waiting to be known.

—Carl Sagan

PRODUCTIVITY AND QUALITY REFLECT MANAGEMENT

We worry a lot these days about productivity and quality control in American industry compared with aggressive foreign competition and, for that matter, our own past. Various causes are said to be behind this situation: a decline in the work ethic, the disenchantment of our youth in the sixties, too much government, and so on. But this condition is far from universal and there are plenty of well-managed American companies whose productivity and quality have not slipped and can hold their own against any in the world.

The truth is there is nothing in the lineup of causes that won't respond to good management in the ways illustrated in this chapter. A business run by complacent, unself-critical management, tends to acquire relaxed standards and cumbersome bureaucratic work habits, which take a heavy toll of performance in all parts of the business.

In approaching a turnaround, there are numerous opportunities for improvement in the area of production strategies, which for our purposes mean not only manufacturing processes but the whole gamut of *administrative work in all areas of the business*, including accounting and control, personnel, engineering, and sales.

PRODUCTIVITY THROUGH WORK SIMPLIFICATION

Work simplification, getting things done with less time and effort, is an easy way to make money, especially in a turnaround situation. But it takes skillful leadership in these ways:

Sell the program to your people

By now they all know the company has problems and must come up with significant improvement in earnings. Get everyone involved in work simplification and sell the idea that work simplification is nothing but *working smarter*. Recognize that activity is not the same as productivity, that everyone may be working hard but not getting the results that will help the company to gain on the competition. Do what you can to protect job security, making payroll savings through attrition and transfers, rather than separations.

Task forces

Start with a task force in one department, composed of management and selected rank-and-file people, operating with written objectives. The task force begins by making up a detailed flowchart of the steps involved in each operation, assigning average time to be taken for each step. The members of the task force solicit suggestions from the people in the department for how the steps in a given operation might be streamlined or simplified. To motivate the people consider a suggestion contest with prizes. Where appropriate, group productivity goals can be effective, with bonuses shared by the members of the group based on improvement.

Stop the paper deluge

When an operation is broken down into all the steps performed along the way, it often becomes self-evident that too many reports are being filled out, too many copies are being made and distributed to too many people, approvals require too many signatures, and too many things require approval unnecessarily. Cumbersome approval habits are a symptom of uncertainty and fear in management, management that is afraid to delegate decisions and responsibility down the line to where they belong. The cure for that is to substitute participative management in which decisions are made at the lowest practical level of the organization and control is exercised not by paralyzing approvals but by reviewing performance against agreed-upon plans and objectives. For example, if Bob Jones is in charge of supplies, he is held responsible for the company's supply expense in relation to written objectives. To require higher-up approval of his ordinary purchases wastes time and money and undermines Bob's effectiveness as an executive. Approvals of this kind are necessary only when the decision involved is of unusual magnitude and rarity, as defined in a written procedure. There is big money to be made in fighting creeping (or galloping) bureaucracy.

Moreover, one should never lose sight of the principle that in any work on productivity there must be clearly maintained standards of quality. Otherwise gains in productivity can be a delusion. For example, if output per man hour is increased 10 percent, but errors increase 15 percent, that is negative progress.

QUALITY CONTROL

When we look back over business history in our generation, we see the powerful impact of expense pressures on the way American business is run. Because of these pressures the whole area of quality standards and controls has been under attack in the name of economy, and one by one standards that used to be considered inviolate have been lowered or eliminated. This used to be called taking a calculated risk, but the risk was either badly calculated or ignored, because we have reached the point where, in too many cases, this kind of expense saving is costing companies more, not less.

When automobile companies recall hundreds of thousands of cars, when food processors and other consumer goods manufacturers have to warn their customers by special announcement not to use products they have bought, and when the collapse of public buildings is no longer an unheard-of event, we must begin to wonder whether it is not time to change quality-control policies that have been so disastrous. Our chief international competitors in Germany and Japan, with their learned American know-how, did not quite follow us on some of these calculated risks, and are scoring competitive points on quality. What is the American consumer's response to all this? As you would expect, there is a hunger for quality goods in the marketplace and it is reflected at the cash register. All of this suggests that there may be a fruitful opportunity for the turnaround company to seek a competitive edge for its products by going after quality.

The road to better quality runs parallel to that of productivity:

Quality control director

Appoint a quality control director, either full-time or part-time, depending on the size of your company. This may not be a permanent job, but for the launching of a new quality-control program, it will help to underline quality as a major company strategy. Having one executive stimulating and monitoring the program will help to advance the ball.

Quality boards

Set up quality boards or committees in each major department, made up of rank-and-file as well as executives. Their mission is to talk out all sides of quality shortfall problems and brainstorm solutions.

Team motivation

Team motivation of each group involved in turning out the product can do a lot to lift quality performance. This involves the setting of goals for the entire group and paying bonuses when they beat the goals or objectives.

Product development

Take a fresh look at product development with a view to researching the costs and benefits of building more quality in the design of the product at the outset.

UPDATE COST ACCOUNTING

Productivity has to do with *efficiency* of output in terms of what is possible. Cost accounting goes on from there to determine the *profitability* of the function. In any competitive field it is essential to have reliable continuing input on the cost of every part of the manufacturing process. Not only is this necessary for accurately gauging the profitability of each item as a guide to your mix strategy, but it is a key ingredient in developing new products to implement your marketing effort. If the in-house accounting forces are not up to the state of the art on this, it may be necessary and worthwhile to have an outside specialist firm help you set up the proper cost-accounting procedures.

Another point: With the upward march of all expenses in an inflationary period, a modern cost-accounting facility can profitably be used on administrative functions as well, to give the management a clearer picture of the cost of things done as a basis for judging whether the result obtained justifies that cost.

THE STRATEGY OF CONCENTRATION

Concentrated efforts are generally more effective—and profitable—than scattered ones. For example, some companies suffer from having too many small plants in different locations. What they may gain in labor supply they can give back many times in the difficulty of recruiting local management for these smaller operations as well as the difficulty of supervising them. And that makes it tough for the company to maintain consistent standards of productivity and quality. A similar principle is involved in lack of concentration in product lines. You make your money on your big items that reflect strong market position and production know-how. In a turnaround situation, therefore, each product line should be carefully appraised with dependable cost-accounting data to encourage a healthy amount of product concentration in the product assortment. This furnishes support for and ties into the mix strategy.

UPDATE EQUIPMENT

While this may not be an early priority in a turnaround, at some point the management needs to review the equipment being used in all phases of production. Assuming that the company is not strapped for capital, it should be looking for ways to spend money in order to make money. The management team should stimulate suggestions for new equipment

that will pay for itself within a reasonable time, say two or
three years, and thereby meet ROI hurdle standards. Companies that do a good job of this wind up with a lower expense
rate. And the converse is true: A company struggling with
obsolete and unproductive equipment is driving with the
brakes on.

RESEARCH AND DEVELOPMENT (R&D)

This also may not be a high up-front priority in a turnaround, but ultimately it is a most important part of production strategy. Again, this is one of America's problems: It is
spending proportionately less on R&D than its best international competitors. Some of the blame for this is said to be that
the current attitude in our financial markets, with analysts
and investors overreacting to temporary dips in earnings, puts
tremendous pressure on management to concentrate on current earnings to the detriment of long-range planning and investment. In certain fields R&D is the lifeblood of the business, and the recruitment and stimulation of top research
talent become a determinant of the future of the business. But
in any industry the search for new approaches and new ways of
doing things is what takes some companies to leadership. In a
turnaround, once management is on its way to getting its
house in order on the fundamentals, it should begin to think
of how best to explore the rich potential of competent research
and development.

31

Financial
Strategies

Knowledge comes, but wisdom lingers.
—Tennyson

Financial policies and strategies play an important role in the life of a company, quite aside from the other management skills. They should, of course, be reflected in the five-year financial plan that is part of the strategic plan (chapter 25).

INFLATION, THE DETERRENT

Under today's conditions financial policy choices have been narrowed from what they used to be. The dangerously high cost of money brought by prolonged inflation makes it increasingly hard to show a return on borrowed capital. This return should normally cover the true or underlying interest

that money is entitled to earn *plus* the expected rate of inflation during the term of the loan. Throughout most of our history inflation has been low to moderate, and therefore required return on investment (ROI) was in an attainable range.
Today required ROI on borrowed capital, with money costs at
record levels, is out of reach for too many companies.

FINANCING THE TURNAROUND

If your company is in a cash-flow and capital squeeze, and
if additional capital must be borrowed to keep the company
going during the turnaround period, here are four suggestions:

1. As part of the strategic plan, prepare a *summary of the
programs* that are expected to bring improved results, and the
length of time it will take. Throw in a contingency factor for
unforseen disappointments, scaling down the projection to a
highly conservative level with a high probability of achievement.

2. From all the programs *select the one expected to bring
the quickest results*, and concentrate on that program as a pilot demonstration of the effectiveness of your whole turnaround plan.

3. Armed with these projections it should be possible to
convince a bank or lending agency with whom you have been
doing business that your undertaking is sound and a good
enough risk to warrant going along with you. Sound lenders
are usually interested in credible turnarounds, especially if
they are members of the same community and therefore have
an emotional interest in the continuity and welfare of your
company.

4. Under today's tight money conditions, some lenders are
negotiating *shared equity as a part of long-term financing*.
This should be done only as a last resort, preferably with buy-
back provisions that would enable the company to regain the
shared equity when earnings and cash flow improve.

CONSERVATIVE ACCOUNTING

As part of your turnaround philosophy you must have financial statements that have the highest credibility based on conservative accounting practices. Not only will this win over possible lenders, but it will save the company from the destructive effects of "happy" statements that turn out not to be true, making things much worse than hitherto reported. This deals a body blow to the all-important morale factor in a turnaround. It is therefore wise to approach a turnaround with a firm policy of viewing the company's situation realistically and conservatively, with accounting providing a candid, unretouched picture. In modern accounting practice there are numerous options of how assets, revenues, and expenses are reported. Choose the more conservative options, for example, the LIFO (last in first out) method of valuing inventories. Also set up adequate reserves for expected losses and known future negative factors affecting earnings. While these measures will report lower earnings, they bring two additional important benefits:

1. They *improve the quality of the the earnings* you will be reporting, thus putting you on the same basis as the best-managed companies.
2. As your earnings improve you will be *saving taxes and helping cash flow.*

FINANCIAL LEVERAGE

Leverage describes the capital structure of the business in terms of the two kinds of capital:

Owned — net worth or equity.
Borrowed — capital obtained through a fixed obligation to repay the borrowed amount at an agreed-upon time, involving short- and long-term debt.

Some companies operate with practically all owned capital
or equity and a negligible amount of debt. Others run with a
substantial amount of debt, sometimes quite successfully. Equity is the company's for keeps and its reward is the company's
earnings. Borrowed capital is in the temporary possession of
the company so long as agreed-upon interest is being paid.

Leveraged financing permits the owners of a business to
have a bigger operation for the capital they put in, in ex-
change for assuming the risk of a debt obligation. If the enterprise is successful they make more on their own investment. If
it is unsuccessful they face greater dangers.

Leverage is illustrated by the following examples, for a
company with a million dollars of total capital:

EXAMPLE A. MEDIUM EARNINGS (20% ON TOTAL CAPITAL BEFORE INTEREST)

	No debt	50% debt, 10% interest	50% debt, 20% interest
Equity	$1,000,000	$500,000	$500,000
Debt	None	$500,000	$500,000
Interest	None	At 10%, $ 50,000	At 20%, $100,000
Net pretax profit	$ 200,000	$150,000 ($200,000 minus $ 50,000)	$100,000 ($200,000 minus $100,000)
% return on equity	$ 200,000 / $1,000,000 / 20%	$150,000 / $500,000 / 30%	$100,000 / $500,000 / 20%

In example A we see that a 20 percent pretax return on equity (ROE) becomes 30 percent if the business is 50 percent
leveraged, that is, half of the total capital is borrowed, and the
interest rate is low (for now) at 10 percent. On the other hand,
a high interest rate of 20 percent produces so much interest expense that it wipes out the leverage effect, and the ROE is the
same 20 percent as it was with no leverage.

Example B shows that the leverage effect of borrowing half
the total capital is greatest when earnings are high as well as

EXAMPLE B. HIGH EARNINGS (30% ON TOTAL CAPITAL BEFORE INTEREST)

	No debt	50% debt, 10% interest	50% debt, 20% interest
Equity	$1,000,000	$500,000	$500,000
Debt	None	$500,000	$500,000
Interest	None	At 10%, $ 50,000	At 20%, $100,000
Net pretax profit	$ 300,000	$250,000 ($300,000 minus $ 50,000)	$200,000 ($300,000 minus $100,000)
% return on equity	$ 300,000 / $1,000,000 / 30%	$250,000 / $500,000 / 50%	$200,000 / $500,000 / 40%

when interest rates are low. In the second column, which combines both these conditions, we see the ROE increased by two-thirds to 50 percent, and even when interest rates are high ROE goes up by one-third.

Example C shows that when earnings are low to moderate, a 50 percent capital leverage is no help to ROE even if interest rates are low, and if interest rates are high operating earnings

EXAMPLE C. LOW EARNINGS (10% ON TOTAL CAPITAL BEFORE INTEREST)

	No debt	50% debt, 10% interest	50% debt, 20% interest
Equity	$1,000,000	$500,000	$500,000
Debt	None	$500,000	$500,000
Interest	None	At 10%, $ 50,000	At 20%, $100,000
Net pretax profit	$ 100,000	$ 50,000 ($100,000 minus $ 50,000)	-0- ($100,000 minus $100,000)
% return on equity	$ 100,000 / $1,000,000 / 10%	$ 50,000 / $ 50,000 / 10%	-0- / -0-

are wiped out and the company may very well be in the red. (In the above examples the interest is assumed to be the average interest paid on all debt)

These examples tell us a good deal about the *leverage aspects in developing a financial strategy*;

1. The attractions of capital leverage have almost been destroyed by high interest rates. In the good old days when the cost of money was about 5 percent, a 50 percent leverage would increase your return on equity—and earnings per share—about 50 percent even if earnings were moderate to low. Under those conditions, that kind of leverage in a stable business might make good sense. But with money costing 4 times what it cost in those days, a 50 percent leverage is ineffective or downright dangerous unless high earnings are assured.

2. Thus high interest rates are particularly hard on turnarounds where a capital injection may be needed to revive a faltering business. This tells us that if you are undertaking a turnaround at a time of high money costs, your first priority should be to improve sales and earnings through better people and better management, and put off capital investment except for items that offer a foolproof high return after the cost of money. High interest rates are a general threat to the growth and profitability of all business, for the same kinds of reasons, because even if a company has an exceptional earnings record, a high capital leverage means sailing with little ballast in a storm, and it becomes difficult for even the best of such companies to take a turndown in earnings. If and when money costs return to more normal levels, capital leverage will again become a consideration in planning a company's financial strategy. But for the present capital investment had better come from cash flow.

CASH FLOW

When money was cheap a company with average earnings had little need to pay much attention to cash flow. Nowadays cash flow consideration is front and center with all but a few of the cash-rich giants. Therefore, performance is measured not only on earnings but also on cash flow, and you have two bottom lines to watch. Cash flow, we have seen, is an essential part of planning and it should be featured in operating reports. Management needs to acquire a heightened awareness of the items on the balance sheet that affect cash flow negatively and positively. Increases in accounts receivable, other receivables, and inventory, hurt cash flow. Increases in accounts payable and other liabilities help cash flow. Operating executives usually need briefing on the dynamics of cash flow, because they are different from the profit flow factors.

With the rise of cash flow concerns, *cash management* has become a field of importance and special emphasis. Cash management has to do with balances maintained in banks, payment timing on accounts payable, bank "floats," and the like.

STANDARDS FOR EXPANSION

In view of the foregoing, top management must handle the whole subject of expansion with unusual caution. Every business needs expansion for growth. But expansion exposes a company to dangers, which need to be properly evaluated. Too many companies have been hurt by injudicious expansion, often fatally. Top management must therefore see to it that every expansion project is backed by careful and conservative projections with a high probability of achievement, that produce a return on investment sufficient to justify going ahead. In other words, the risk-gain ratio must be clearly favorable.

ASSET MANAGEMENT

Part of the turnaround process is an evaluation of the effectiveness of each component of the company's assets in contributing to the company's earnings and growth. There have been a number of turnarounds where a company with low capital availability has recognized that certain of its assets did not ideally fit the company's mission. Another way of putting this is that the management feels that the value of those questionable assets could be put to better use as a capital injection into the company's most attractive growth opportunities. Selling those assets in today's market can usually be expected to produce a premium over book value as well as provide the needed capital. In short, asset management can be approached in much the same way as trend marketing and mix strategies, because it is shaping the company for better growth and profits in response to its strengths, weaknesses, opportunities, and threats.

MERGERS AND ACQUISITIONS

In turnaround situations mergers and acquisitions can offer possibilities of strengthening the company in one of the following ways:

1. Providing more concentration by filling gaps in markets.
2. Rounding out the company's product mix by adding new products with high potential.
3. Providing diversification to fill a perceived need.
4. Helping the company to build a new image.

A turnaround company cannot afford an acquisition that adds to its problems. Therefore, to be helped and not hurt by an acquisition program, your turnaround management should look to three requirements:

1. *That the acquisition under consideration fits* into what has been decided upon as the company's mission.
2. *That the company being acquired is well-managed,* has a promising future as it stands, and that its management will remain in place under the proposed merger.
3. *That the merger can be accomplished without dangerously affecting the company's financial position.* The

price of a merger, like any other price, is determined by supply and demand, and demand is affected by waves of preference that are much like fashions. In general, if an acquisition target fills all the requirements from your point of view, price should not be the controlling factor, providing you can afford it, and should be looked at on a long-term basis. Where an aggressive management, as recommended above, will continue to run the company, it may be wise for the acquiring company in its turnaround situation to work out a performance payout deal, where the acquired management is paid partly in future amounts tied to profit performance. This has the double advantage of, on the one hand, easing the immediate problem of paying for the acquisition, and at the same time providing the newly enriched acquired management with a strong incentive to continue hitting the ball.

PART VI

Motivating
the Team
(The Fuel)

A man can succeed at almost anything for which he has unlimited enthusiasm.
                                    —Charles M. Schwab

32

Motivation
Builders

*Leadership: the art of getting others to want to
do what you feel should be done.*
—Vance Packard

BRINGING OUT ACTION POTENTIAL

We have now covered much of the terrain of a typical turnaround: getting mentally geared up for the turnaround, working out the bifocal plans, agreeing on the strategies. It is now time to focus on *development of the individual*, what management can do to bring out the full action potential of each person on the team, or, using Vance Packard's words, what top management can do to get all team members to pull together and *want* to do what the leaders feel should be done. This is the essence of motivation, that complex and powerful force that can determine the destiny of a business. If we were to do a scientific sampling of all the people, rank-and-file and executive, in American companies, ranking, on the one hand, their inherent physical and mental ability and, on the other, their actual on-the-job performance, we would find that the range from worst to best in inherent ability is much less than the range from worst to best in actual performance.

This says that the same kind of people will do much better working in one company than they will in another, or in one department of a company than they will in another. The reason for this is that man, being an emotional animal, performs to a large extent based on how he *feels*.

ABILITY TO GET ABOVE-AVERAGE RESULTS WITH AVERAGE PEOPLE

Leadership can in fact be judged by its ability to get above-average results with average people. Let's take a look at seven things that affect the building of motivation in a company:

The death of command authority

As a chief executive officer, you have the power to hire and fire your people, but you had better not think you have much real *command* authority. In our society the traditional command authority that used to exist in the family, in the school, in the church, has dwindled to the point where the power of the person "in command" is based mostly on persuasion, not command. This wholesome outgrowth of a democratic society is at work in business as well, where the old-fashioned command-authority boss often is not getting the job done, while the leader-teacher-persuader is. In the end strong people will not put up with an authoritarian command environment, although weak people may knuckle under to stay on the payroll. In Abraham Maslow's words, if all you have is a hammer you tend to treat everything as a nail. And nails don't move unless driven.

Negative emotions cancel action

When an individual is deeply upset he cannot work well. Therefore, a supervisor who gets his people upset is turning off performance. Members of the team who have a street fighter's approach (like David Merrick's crack, "It's not enough that I should succeed—others should fail") can be brilliant high achievers themselves, but they inevitably lower the group performance.

Participative management releases energy

Years ago the famous Hawthorne experiment opened our eyes to this fact. Two completely similar groups in a Western Electric plant were involved, one of which was told that the management had selected them for an important series of experimental changes in their working conditions, while the other group was told nothing and was kept as an unchanged control for comparison purposes. As each of a series of improvements in working conditions was introduced, the output of the experimental group kept going up. But to the amazement of the researchers, when these improvements were one by one removed again output *still* kept going up. The moral: The all-important factor that motivated improved performance was that the people in the experimental group felt excited about being singled out for an important experiment. This meant more than the impersonal improvement in working conditions. Thus a work environment where people participate in problem solving and decision making stimulates the will to achieve and releases energy.

Communication skills

Therefore, a first prerequisite in building motivation in a turnaround company is for its leadership to develop and apply communication skills with its people. Some people seem to grow up with these skills, but many otherwise effective executives suffer from a lack of knowledge and training in this area. But because interpersonal communication skills are at the heart of getting results through people, it will really pay the turnaround manager to learn all he can about them. Good seminars, courses, and books are readily available (see chapter 13). The following eight suggestions have been found helpful, particularly in turnaround situations:

1. *High visibility of top management.* Top management that is not often seen is at a disadvantage from a communications standpoint. People wonder what the boss is like, and the answers that come from scuttlebutt are rarely complimentary. Moreover, people fear the unknown, and invisibility aggravates the normal tendency of employees to be afraid of the boss.

2. A *democratic atmosphere* helps communication. While the boss understandably has a larger office and other perks, he should not be flaunting a baronial life-style while the rest of the organization lives like peasants.

3. *Consideration for others* should be evident in the boss's everyday deportment. He should not keep people waiting, either in his outer office when they have an appointment or when they are in his office and he talks on the telephone. Some top management executives fall into the habit of sending for people at any time, without notice, when most of the time the question to be asked could have waited for an answer until a regularly planned meeting or could have been handled in a telephone call. This sets an inconsiderate example for the whole organization. When an impromptu get-together has to be called, a word of apology is in order. In contrast with this demotivating the-boss-has-me-on-a-string feeling, it helps to warm up relationships when the boss goes to the subordinate's office for a meeting. It is also good office manners, when there is a meeting in the boss's office, to sit around a table, so that the boss is not enthroned behind the largest and cleanest desk in the company.

4. *Correctional technique.* One of the most difficult things for the busy top executive to handle properly is a situa-

tion where he is disturbed by something wrong. All too often this results in an outbreak of spur-of-the-moment criticism of the culprit in front of others. This is guaranteed to lower morale and destroy motivation. The good leader does not express displeasure in public, and, in fact, avoids judgmental comments about an individual. Critical personal comments are wounding to the recipient and not soon forgotten. And yet the boss cannot sidestep his responsibility of dealing with situations that need correction. This is where Management By Objectives is a great help, because it focuses attention on self-appraisal of performance and rescues the boss from the role of unilateral judge of the subordinate. A simple and effective solution to the correctional problem is to use questions instead of statements, that is, to ask the subordinate what he thinks about the situation. This will usually elicit an honest self-appraisal of what went wrong and how it will be corrected, along with a feeling of admiration for the boss's tact and skill in managing without injury to feelings.

5. *One-on-one meetings*. A valuable technique that is efficient and builds mutual esteem and team spirit is a regular weekly meeting of the CEO with each of the people who report to him. This is at an agreed-upon time, and it is the *subordinate's meeting* in which he brings up matters he has saved for discussion with the boss. The boss lets the subordinate take the lead and when the latter is finished with his items the CEO brings up whatever is on his list. Many chief executives feel that such a meeting is unnecessary because they see their people all the time anyway. But from the employee's standpoint there is a big difference between being perpetually at the boss's beck and call and having his own regular meeting time when he has the boss's ear. It takes a little self-discipline on the boss's part to set up and adhere to a regular meeting schedule of this kind, but it is worth the effort, and it is a proven top management technique widely used in successful companies, not only for the CEO but as a method of managing at all levels.

6. *Inspirational meetings*. Especially in a turnaround situation, a dramatic and effective way for a chief executive to communicate accurately with the whole team is in large inspi-

rational meetings, carefully planned and well executed. In this setting the organization hears from its top leadership the course that has been set for the company and how they are moving along that course. Participation by middle management reporting success stories is a good way to build self-confidence and firm up everyone's determination to achieve company goals.

7. *Off-premises talk-outs*. For small groups where synergistic problem solving is the agenda, brainstorming sessions out of the office are an excellent way to come up with the best group thinking and also build team spirit and group motivation.

8. *Memorandums and letters*. Some busy executives go through their reports (often before anyone else has them) and fire off critical notes to the day's culprits who don't look good in the figures. The one who gets such a note is apt to resent it, particularly if the only time he hears from the boss in writing is in one of these needling, nit-picking missives. A good communications rule, strongly recommended by long experience, is never to write a letter or memorandum that will upset the recipient. When you have probing or correcting to do, do it orally *in private*. When there is something *good* to be said, *write a letter*. This written pat on the back (with copies to others where appropriate) will not only boost the morale and motivation of all concerned, but will be kept by the recipient, sometimes for years. And be sure that you do enough praising. The top executive who spends most of his time assigning the blame will never build motivation.

Leadership in adversity

When all is said and done, perhaps the best morale builder is group success. When business is good and the company is well ahead of its objectives, top management has few morale or motivational problems, but when business is tough and the whole organization is fighting in the trenches, leadership is really on trial. That is when top management needs self-discipline to avoid carping, grousing, and lashing out at whoever is in reach. This lack of self-control tells the team that the boss is worried and insecure. They know that things are not good and what they need is to have the boss cheer them up and register confidence. The leader who is human and warm (but not soft) when the going is difficult wins the kind of loyalty that is not soon forgotten.

Management development office

The management development function of the personnel arm of the business has a key role to play in motivation. No matter how small the company, someone in personnel should have the special responsibility for monitoring and stimulating morale and motivation. Beginning with the recruiting effort, through the training period, appraisal sessions, down to the exit interview, at all these steps the awareness of the level of motivation in the company and the process of raising it should be in sharp focus. One of the techniques that may be very helpful in a turnaround situation is the employee opinion survey, in which people at all levels of the business answer an unsigned, detailed questionnaire about how they feel on a long list of matters relating to their morale and motivation (see chapter 11).

Compensation

Clearly a most direct and powerful builder of motivation is a compensation structure based on results achieved. Whether in straight salary, bonuses, or special contests, money talks to each team member who, if he is a good achiever in business, is equally determined to achieve a good personal and family life for which he has pretty clear financial objectives. And that leads us to the best available answer to the whole compensation question: Management By Objectives.

33

Management By Objectives (MBO)

*The deepest principle of human nature is the
craving to be appreciated.*

—William James

MBO AS A MONEY-MAKER

Of all the management philosophies and techniques that
have developed in our times, one stands out for its effectiveness and breadth of application: Management By Objectives.
But it should be made clear at the outset that when we talk of
MBO we mean a multifaceted professional management system that is properly implemented throughout the organization
in such a way as to produce maximum motivation and results.
In American business today, most companies work with goals
and objectives in one way or another, and many say they are

on MBO. But relatively few companies have put the necessary time and effort into installing the detailed procedures of MBO and indoctrinating their entire team in *how to use MBO to make money* for the company and each team member. These methods will be covered in the next chapters, but first, in order to justify the substantial time and effort that MBO involves, let's look at the broad values as well as some of the pitfalls of MBO.

WHAT IS MBO?

Management By Objectives is a professional management technique for maximizing individual and company performance through a participative effort between each team member and his boss to agree on clearly defined, short-term performance objectives that reflect the individual's job responsibilities and standards of performance in the light of the company's objectives, and that are self-appraised by the individual and reviewed by his boss and higher management, as a basis for compensation and promotion.

HOW MBO BUILDS MORALE

Think back to the first day on your first job. You come to work, excited by the adventure of a new life and the dreams of opportunity. Mixed with this enthusiasm is suppressed apprehension about how you will get along in a new environment with all those strange people. If you were lucky the apprehension melted away and the enthusiasm lasted and grew. But perhaps, as time went on, all of your job relationships were not entirely harmonious, your boss was uncommunicative, and you began to wonder how you were doing and where you stood. When enthusiasm is replaced by trauma, doubts grow and performance suffers.

Here are seven ways in which MBO fights such morale erosion.

Clarity versus doubt

The worst part of the example just described is the gnaw-
ing doubt, not knowing if you are doing what you are expected
to, and how "they" feel you are doing. With the proper MBO
setup, you have a written *job description* that clearly spells out
your responsibilities, and you have written *standards of performance* on each of those responsibilities. Then you have a
set of *performance objectives* for the current year, which you
wrote and which, in your opinion, were the most important
things you were to accomplish this year. These objectives were
reviewed with your boss, who approved them with a few minor
changes. You talk to your boss every three months or so about
how you are doing on each objective, and at the end of the
year you write a self-appraisal of your performance, which is
discussed at length with your boss, after which he responds
with his acceptance or suggested modification of your appraisal. This passes up through management channels and is
reflected in your compensation and career path.

Just as if you were a member of a professional football
team, you know what position you are playing, you know the
rules of the game, your performance is clearly quantified, and
at contract time you know that how much you are paid depends on what you do with the ball. In professional football
motivation has to be at its highest, hence Vince Lombardi's
more than half-serious remark: "If you aren't fired with enthusiasm, you'll be fired with enthusiasm."

MBO not only clarifies the what, when, and how of your
performance, but it leaves no doubt as to who your boss is. It is
not at all uncommon for an individual to feel that he is an-
swerable to too many bosses. Under MBO he knows that his
boss is the one who works with him on his objectives and performance appraisals as well as compensation.

Less nagging and assigning of blame

Without MBO the typical executive coping with all the
problems of a troubled company is apt to think that his main

job is hopping on things that go wrong, and "straightening out" whoever is to blame. In that kind of picture lots of things, often the same things, go wrong, and the team-member goes home at night and tells his wife about the carping attitude and continual nagging he is getting from his boss, and that he is getting blamed for things that are not entirely his fault. With MBO the nagging stops when the objectives are written. The boss says, "Look, Joe, we have had a lot of trouble with objective three, and that has to stop. You have taken it as an objective and I am confident you can make it. I'm not going to yell at you or needle you, the objective itself takes care of that. But you and I know that this objective is vitally important and that in the long run if you don't make it, it will hurt your future with the company."

Activity versus accomplishment

Without MBO the team members can be working hard putting out fires and doing what they are told, and yet there may be no clear connection between all that work and the end result in company performance. With MBO the most important wanted results for the company are translated into individual written objectives for each team member. When he goes home at night he can think over what he did today and whether and how much it advanced the ball on his objectives. It therefore becomes clear to the individual and the management how much nonobjective activity is going on so it can be minimized.

Rewards for results

When a good MBO system has become a way of life in a company you get results-oriented management from top to bottom. All team members know that their performance is rated on the management development charts each year, and that the best increases and promotions go to the 7s or over on a scale of 10, and not the 3s or 4s. This is motivation at its height.

Maturity and respect

MBO has a very constructive effect on the whole subordi-nate-supervisor relationship. The subordinate feels he is being treated with respect because he is asked to write his own objec-tives and his own self-appraisal. He is working as a member of a participative management, and when he goes to work in the morning he knows exactly what it is he is trying to accomplish and how he is doing. The childish and emotional behavior that sometimes creeps into the subordinate-supervisor rela-tionship has been filtered out, its place taken by mature inter-action.

How MBO gets results

In addition to providing a high degree of motivation, MBO works for getting results in three ways:

Action program. In support of each major objective, a professional MBO system requires a written action program for achieving it. This program is reviewed with the supervisor, and, if necessary, the design of the program is helped by staff specialists. The individual must feel that it is his program, re-viewed with and approved by his boss, and that both are con-vinced the program is the best way to achieve the objective.

Checkpoints. When the objective is written, dates are es-tablished as checkpoints during the year, at which time the team member reviews progress with his boss. At this "touch base" session, problems are aired, suggestions discussed, and, if advisable, outside staff help obtained.

Renegotiation. If conditions change during the year it may be desirable and fair to revise a performance objective either up or down depending on changed circumstances. For exam-ple, if a new government regulation or a major strike drasti-cally affects the achievement of an objective, the latter is amended to reflect these unforeseen changes. Failing this, an understanding is reached that the changed conditions will be taken into consideration at the performance appraisal at the end of the year.

MBO, real or plastic?

The only way to find the answer to this question is to leave the front office and talk to the people on the receiving end of MBO, those in middle management.

MBO is plastic when they say:

"Yeah, we have MBO. My boss writes out my objectives and gives them to me, and I have them somewhere in my desk, but nobody seems to look at them or talk about them, and my boss never mentions them until he hands me next year's. Anyway, they're really not *my* objectives, they're *his*. He wrote them."

or

"We go through the motions of writing objectives, but they don't mean anything because nobody ever talks to us about them. I guess it's one of those things you do in a big company."

or

"I like MBO, and we work out our objectives pretty well with the boss, but then at the end of the year he rates us on what we did, and we never have a chance to talk to him about it. I think some of the time his ratings are unfair, and that turns me off on the whole MBO idea."

MBO is real when they say:

"MBO is a lot of work, but I really like it. I feel as if I'm part of a team that's working together to do better for the company and ourselves. The first year our objectives were kind of vague and hard to measure, but by now they really spell out what it is I am trying to do in my job. And I know how I'm doing because I talk over my programs with the boss three or four times a year. To tell you the truth, MBO has helped me a lot with the boss. He's tough but he's fair, and he treats us like human beings and partners, not machines. Instead of telling us what to do all the time, he lets us come up with the answers. He's become a pretty good listener and we all know what the score is as far as getting ahead is concerned. MBO has been a great help. I'm all for it."

34

How to Make MBO Produce

Miracles happen only to those who believe in them.

—French proverb

CHANGING STATES OF MIND

How much truth there is in that old proverb, and how strongly it applies to turnarounds! The discouragement and disappointment one lives with in an ailing company make it exceedingly difficult to change prevailing states of mind from negative to positive, from skepticism to belief in the company's revival. This is why a whole new approach to life in the company, involving everyone in a new way of approaching his job, is recommended in the form of Management By Objectives.

MBO is not easy to put into a company and make it really produce as a results-getting technique. Explained to people for the first time it has plenty of appeal, and they like the idea of participative goal setting and participative performance appraisal. But when they begin to realize how much time it takes to learn how to write objectives and do appraisals and then for each team member to talk out his objectives and performance with his boss at each level of management, all on a predetermined time schedule, you can expect some grousing and some questions about whether there aren't more important things to be done then all this "professional management."

MBO, A KEY TURNAROUND STRATEGY

And yet, MBO working properly can do more than anything else to change doubters into believers who can bring new results to the company.

Therefore, in your turnaround situation, whether you have never worked with MBO or have a more or less plastic version, you cannot afford to ignore the potential of MBO as a turnaround strategy. And once you, as management, are sold, you must be sure that you sell the concept to the organization.

SELLING THE MBO STRATEGY TO YOUR PEOPLE

CEO leadership

This is a job that cannot be done without the CEO. The head of the business must believe in it and put over his enthusiasm to the full management team. His script:

1. MBO is used by many of the star-performing companies in most industries.
2. MBO will not only help each of you to do better and enjoy your work more, but will also help to develop you in your career.
3. It clears up what each of us is trying to do and how he is doing, better than any other system.
4. You will be asked more and told less as a result of participative management.

5. To get the full benefit of MBO requires a lot of energy and time, and it will work for us as it does in so many top-performing companies. I believe in it and I expect you to follow through enthusiastically. Your investment in time and effort will pay off for you and for the company.

CEO training

To insure the CEO's involvement and support of the MBO program, it is a good idea for the CEO himself to begin the process by taking a professional management course on the outside. In all too many cases where companies decide to put in MBO, the CEO delegates the job to a subordinate and is "too busy" to get personally involved. This example of low urgency set at the top is apt to be echoed all along the line, and such an MBO launching has a poor chance of success. On the other hand, the fact that the head of the company devotes his time to a professional management seminar will not only broaden his horizons but will also tell everybody on the team that the new MBO strategy is a high priority for all team members.

Compensation tied to MBO

An announcement from the CEO that compensation will ultimately be tied into the MBO process and reflect performance against objectives will go a long way in selling the program.

Training seminars

It should also be explained that MBO is a complicated participative system and that the company does not expect to reach top professional form in the first year. It is then appropriate to announce a training program with group seminars for the purpose of teaching all participants their part in the process.

COMPONENTS OF MBO

There are four parts to the MBO process:

1. Job description
2. Standards of performance
3. Objectives
4. Performance appraisal

Job description

Remembering that clarity is one of the keys to successful management by objectives, we must begin by making sure that each individual and his boss agree on just what that individual's job is. If there are two different ideas about what the job covers, effective management is derailed right there. The job description should spell out the areas:

1. *To whom the executive reports*, whom he supervises, and with whom he works.
2. A clear statement of the *main functions of the position*, what someone going into that job is supposed to do.
3. A numbered *list of the responsibilities* of the position that carry out the previously described functions.

Anyone going into an executive job should be expected to have a hand in the writing of his job description, after first discussing it with his boss and perhaps the personnel head. If there is an existing job description, he suggests any changes that seem advisable. He then reviews his draft with his boss and arrives at an agreed-upon job description that will apply to him. The personnel head will see to it that all job descriptions follow a similar format.

Standards of performance

Now that the job responsibilities have been spelled out, the next logical step is to clarify what standard of performance is expected in each of those responsibilities. When companies

leave out standards of performance they lose a valuable opportunity to tell the new jobholder at the outset what the company expects as a continuing standard of performance on each
of his responsibilities. When the standards are omitted the
employee works with a job description and his objectives,
which are short-range and few in number. The standards of
performance cover a broader list of activities and are open-
ended in time.

A standard of performance for any job represents the level
of excellence for a particular function that the management
considers reasonably attainable in the long run. The objective, on the other hand, is what the management expects to
achieve in the current year in the light of all circumstances,
and this may not be up to the standard of ultimate performance. For example, suppose the job description outlines responsibility for quality control in a certain operation. Based
on what is being achieved in the industry as well as the company's potential, the standard of performance might be that rejections for quality defects shall not exceed 3 percent. But if
quality control has been a grave problem in this instance and
rejections have recently been running 15 percent, the negotiated *objective* for the current year might be 8 percent, with
the idea that the 3 percent standard will be reached next year
or the year after. It is a good idea to include the standards of
performance on the job description divided into two columns,
the area of responsibility in the first column, followed by the
standard of performance in the second, thus:

Responsibility	Standard of Performance Reached
I am responsible for quality control in my division.	When rejects do not exceed 3 percent of the total.

Writing objectives and action programs

Armed with the job description and standards of performance, the executive is now in a position to begin work on his
objectives for the year ahead. Here are some guidelines:

Objectives defined. An objective is one of a short list of the
most desired results expected to be achieved during the year.

Ask yourself, "What is the most important measurable result I have to make happen this year?" Then go on to the next most important desired results.

Company objectives. The executive writes objectives for his accomplishment during the year within the framework of what the company as a whole expects to accomplish in that period. The first step, therefore, is for top management to develop the *company* objectives and communicate them in a series of meetings to the next levels of managment. At each level the executive in charge then develops suggested objectives for the *group* reporting to him, in line with the company's total objectives. These group objectives are then communicated to the members of the group as a guide for preparation of their own objectives. Group or company objectives should not be allowed to inhibit the individual from thinking through and expressing what he feels are the most important results to be accomplished *in his job*. The heart of the MBO process is participation and interaction between each executive and his boss. Management must see to it that the two-way process really works, with top-down input really interacting with and adjusting to vigorous bottom-up input.

Less is more. It is better to have a few dynamite objectives with a powerful call to action than a long shopping list with diluted attention and effort. One of the most frequent first-year mistakes in a new MBO program is that people, in their zeal to leave no stone unturned, wind up with fifteen or twenty objectives. The whole point of MBO is to get your key goals to the forefront of your consciousness so that daily awareness will lead to continuous effort. When MBO is effective, the executive can, at any time, reel off his objectives by heart. With fifteen objectives that doesn't happen, and the executive, while he may be proud of the impressive number of objectives in his file, does not go to work in the morning with a clear mental picture of his main mission. Experience suggests, therefore, that five or six key objectives are plenty, at least for the first few years.

A second frequent malfunction in beginning MBO programs is "motherhood" objectives, in which the goal is so general as to have little to do with important results this year.

Equally to be avoided are objectives that talk about work instead of results: "I will make every effort to improve quality performance," or "Develop a program for improving quality performance," instead of "Rejects will not exceed 8 percent." In the rare instances where building the program is itself a massive undertaking of the highest priority, it is a valid objective, but most of the time what the company needs is results, and while the program is intended to get the results, it is a *support system* and not an objective.

Statistical and nonstatistical. The first objective is usually a compilation of the statistical results expected, sales, profit, and other operating figures regularly reported. The other objectives cover nonstatististical results desired, and these should be:

1. Serious problem areas that urgently need correction and meet the test of being among the five or six things most important to be accomplished in the coming year.
2. Nonstatistical objectives should be couched in *measurable terms*, and while this takes some ingenuity, it can usually be done. For example, if the objective is to update the look of the packaging, it may specify that the new packaging is to be judged within the top three in the industry by a qualified group. There is no need to be overly concerned about the problem of measuring performance on an objective that seems hard to quantify. In actual experience there are always reliable opinions to be had, and at appraisal time there is rarely much difference of opinion.

Action programs. Each objective should be backed up with a written program of action for its achievement. Some companies use a two-column form for written objectives, in which the left-hand column describes the objective and the right-hand column a summary of the program. In addition, on the far right there is a space for suggested review dates and the completion date where appropriate (see Table 7).

Review with the boss. When the executive takes his objectives to his boss for review, the boss's main function is to see

TABLE 7.

GENERAL TURNAROUNDS, INC.

Name _____

Position _____

Date _____

For Year _____

O B J E C T I V E S

No.	Objective	Action Program	Dates	
			Review	Completion

that the most important *desired results* are in the objectives, and to weed out unnecessary or "motherhood" objectives or those that are taken for granted as part of the job description. He must also see to it that the objectives are achievable, not too soft and not too hard, and that they tie into the group and company objectives.

Procedure and timing. Depending on the size of the company, the objective-setting process takes four to eight weeks near the end of the fiscal year, in the following steps:

Step 1: Top management develops company objectives and reviews them with the board of directors, if appropriate.

Step 2: Top management communicates the company objectives at a staff meeting.

Step 3: Each executive in the next layer of management develops his individual objectives and forwards them to his boss.

Step 4: Top management reviews these individual objectives.

Step 5: Top management meets separately with each reporting executive to agree on objectives, action plans, and measurement standards.

Step 6: The second layer of management executives each hold staff meetings with their immediate subordinates to communicate their unit's objectives (similar to step 2).

Next steps: Repeat steps 3 to 5 down to the lowest management level on MBO.

On introducing MBO for the first time it is usually desirable to limit the first-year installation to the top few executive layers, broadening the process to include all executives in the following year or two.

35

Appraisal of Performance

I was successful because you believed in me.
—Ulysses S. Grant to Abraham Lincoln

THE KEY PART OF THE MBO PROCESS

The most productive and constructive part of the whole range of work relationships in a company is the year-end review or performance appraisal. Thousands of potentially good people work for dominant-hostile (Q1) bosses who turn the review into a monologue of criticism and threat; or for a Q2 boss whom they very seldom see and from whom they receive little candor or real help; or for a Q3 boss who pats them on the back and rambles on without coming to a useful point.

But in a professionally managed business under dominant-warm (Q4) leadership, the review is the moment of truth when the employee becomes the subject of a private meeting with his employer, the outcome of which will affect his livelihood and his future. Depending on how the boss behaves, the employee can leave the meeting stimulated, excited about his job, and happily sold on the company, or he can come away bitter about his boss's unfairness, hostility, or lack of understanding, feeling that he made a mistake in joining the company and ought to put out his résumé in the job market. Clearly, the performance appraisal part of MBO can make it or break it. Unless the management is prepared to devote the necessary time, thought, and coaching to the appraisal process, it had better not attempt to install Management By Objectives in the company.

APPRAISAL GUIDELINES

To make appraising performance a positive factor in a company's management, these guidelines have been helpful:

The boss listens

MBO without self-appraisal defeats its purpose of getting better results through *participative* management. The only way to get good self-appraisals is to make the subordinate feel like a partner, not a victim, and to open him up by being a good listener. Training high achievers to be good listeners is not easy, and action always speaks louder than words. In addition to plenty of coaching for the executive staff on this important point, the chief executive and top management must set an example to the rest of the organization by demonstrating they are good listeners in the reviews they handle.

The appraisal is rating the performance, not the person

For example, an executive may be a number 8 in all-around ability, but in a new and difficult assignment may perform at a number 5 level in the first year. Moreover, the performance must be judged against the environment in which it took place. Suppose that, since the objective was written, there has been a dramatic collapse in the industrywide market involving a certain objective. The executive may have missed achieving the objective and still have done an outstanding job compared to competition, thus deserving a high rating. The converse is true when unexpected change brings a windfall that produces exceptional results. Performance against the written objectives is, of course, the major concern of the appraisal. But in the appraisal some consideration should also be given to performance against the job responsibilities set forth in the job description that are not covered by objectives.

Promotability

In addition to rating current performance, the management needs to know another thing about the employee, and that is his promotability, present and future. It is therefore well to include in the appraisal process a rating of the individual's advancement potential or promotability, to what level and when.

Scale of 10

For reasons mentioned in earlier chapters, the scale of 10 as a rating system has a number of advantages: It cannot be misunderstood, it forces more precise thinking in the appraisal, and it pictures the level of performance so dramatically that it motivates improvement. Before the appraisal work is started, the management should establish what rating is to be given to barely achieving the objective. Ideally, in a high-performing organization, achieving objectives is what executives are being paid to do and so they should get a midpoint rating, like a 5 or a 6, with higher ratings assigned when they beat the objective moderately (7 or 8) or explosively (9 or 10).

Overall rating

Since objectives are not of equal importance to the company, the executive in his self-appraisal should take into account the relative importance of each objective in arriving at an overall rating for his total performance. This should be made clear in his discussion with his boss, when any differences of opinion should be negotiated to the point of agreement.

The atmosphere of the meeting

Maintaining the proper atmosphere is important for the success of the meeting. The boss should set aside at least two hours for the meeting, turn off phone calls, and make an effort to achieve a quiet, relaxed environment. Throughout the organization appraisal meetings should be considered of the utmost importance, the dates should be set well in advance, with copies to top managment so that conflicting meetings are not called and appraisal meetings are not canceled or postponed.

STAGES OF THE APPRAISAL PROCESS

To get the best results from participative MBO performance appraisal, shortcuts must be avoided and these six basic steps followed:

Preparation

As part of the training in MBO the executive receives coaching on the writing of a self-appraisal of his performance against his objectives. Also, at the time the objectives are set for the next year his boss gives him the dates for the self-appraisal discussion, the appraisal interview, and one or more progress reviews during the year. The executive is given to understand that he writes up his appraisal of results on each objective in advance and comes to the self-appraisal meeting prepared to tell his boss how he sees his performance during the past year on the objectives as well as on other responsibilities of his job. Before this meeting the boss will have read the executive's self-appraisal, compared it with his standards of performance, and jotted down a list of questions for him to use to keep the executive speaking freely.

The self-appraisal meeting

Properly briefed, the boss is determined to devote this meeting to listening. Under no circumstances does he make critical comments or take the subordinate to task. The subordinate naturally comes to the meeting well supplied with anxiety and even fear, so that he may not be at his best as a communicator, worrying more about the boss's reactions than about his own presentation. If the meeting can be held in the subordinate's office that will help. In any case, the boss should not be sitting at his big desk, like a judge, with the subordinate in the prisoner's docket. Questions rather than statements from the boss will be helpful; for example, "How do you feel we are working together?"; "How can I help you to do a better job?"; "Are you aware of obstacles or needs that you have in your job?"; "Let's talk about your personal growth." If this self-appraisal meeting is handled thoughtfully and expertly by the boss, the subordinate will leave feeling that it was a fine experience, that he had the boss's full attention and was treated with consideration, fairness, and as an equal.

The boss's appraisal

This should be written right after the self-appraisal meeting, while the details are still fresh in the boss's mind. It should cover performance against objectives, other accomplishments during the year, general strengths and weaknesses, and promotional potential. The boss's appraisal should show the subordinate's self-appraisal for each item as well as his, and comment on any differences of rating. Where MBO is working well, with participative work progress discussions during the year, the differences in appraisal should be few and far between. Indeed, strong performers are often more critical about their own performance than their boss is apt to be. Conversely, it is the weak performer that wears rose-colored glasses.

Discussion with the next level

A necessary sequel to this is that the boss reviews his written appraisal of each of his subordinates with his own supervisor at the next higher level. This enables top management to try to get consistency in ratings throughout the organization and level out the tendencies of some people to rate too leniently and others too critically. It also provides a valuable opportunity to monitor how the self-appraisal meetings—the key to a good MBO operation—are being handled. In this review salary and bonus recommendations are presented and the objectives for next year covered.

The appraisal interview

When the salary and bonus decisions have been finalized, the subordinate meets with his boss for the appraisal wrap-up. The boss explains any differences between his appraisal and the subordinate's, discusses problems and programs for improvement, reviews the objectives for the next year, and makes every effort to arrive at a meeting of the two minds on the total performance appraisal and compensation decision.

STEPS IN THE APPRAISAL PROCESS

Whereas the objective-writing process is triggered at the top with the company objectives, the appraisal process *begins at the bottom* and works its way up.

Step 1: At the lowest level in the MBO program, each executive writes his self-appraisal and forwards it to his supervisor.

Step 2: The self-appraisal discussion between the two takes place.

Step 3: The supervisors of first-level executives write appraisals after each self-appraisal meeting.

Step 4: The supervisor discusses these appraisals with his boss and the next level above.

Step 5: The first supervisor conducts appraisal interviews with each of his subordinates.

Step 6: The first supervisor writes his own self-appraisal and forwards it to his boss.

From then on similar steps are repeated up to the highest management level.

MANAGEMENT-BUILDING FOLLOW-THROUGH

Each executive's overall performance rating as well as his promotional potential rating should appear on an organization planning chart with a box for each of the team members under each group supervisor. This chart gives management a clear picture of the organization, how each team member is doing, his age and length of service, compensation and promotability. Once developed, this organizational planning chart has many uses, including the identification of replacement candidates for openings as they occur (see Table 8).

TABLE 8. ORGANIZATION PLANNING CHART

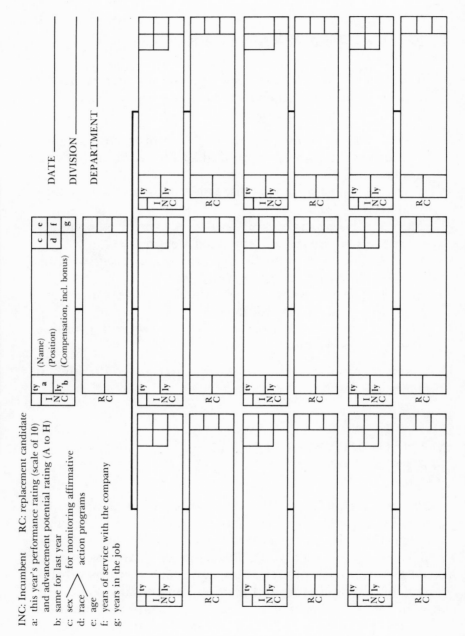

INC: Incumbent   RC: replacement candidate

a: this year's performance rating (scale of 10)
   and advancement potential rating (A to H)

b: same for last year

c: sex ⟩ for monitoring affirmative

d: race ⟩ action programs

e: age

f: years of service with the company

g: years in the job

DATE _____

DIVISION _____

DEPARTMENT _____

226

As was said earlier, this has been a lot of work, but big rewards call for big efforts. And in MBO we are playing for big stakes: seeking a turnaround in the team's motivation, a turnaround in productivity, a resultant turnaround in the bottom line, and along with that, building a winning team.

36

How to
Get More Done

*If I have done the public any service, it is due to
patient thought.*

—Sir Isaac Newton

WASTED EXECUTIVE TIME

Low productivity is not just a problem of the production
line; it applies to executives on a broad scale. Because their
hourly production is not measured, we have no idea of the tremendous cost of wasted managerial time. Even though the
man with superior action skills should tend to rise to the top in
our system, there are all too many companies where top management itself sets a poor example of time effectiveness, which
seeps through the company. And the chances are that in a
turnaround situation, there is real pay dirt in tackling wasted
time and motion at all executive levels.

THREE PRINCIPLES

To reap that harvest, all members of the executive team should accept and cultivate three prime movers in the art of getting things done:

Self-management

The executive who approaches his job with the ambition to be a high achiever must be happily self-critical and demand self-discipline. His first responsibility is to manage himself, because if he cannot control what he does he won't control what his people do.

Belief in interaction

Management is getting results *through people*. Therefore the effective manager cultivates the ability to maximize the results achieved by the team under his responsibility. He should not think: "In my job I will do as much as possible." He should think: "In my job I will *get done* as much as possible."

Planning begets doing

Many executives feel they must be on the go all the time, and tests have shown that most think they spend more time planning than they actually do. Yet it is a proven principle that more planning time *reduces* the total time needed to achieve an objective. This is the rationale behind the MBO strategy and it applies with equal force to the whole gamut of running a business.

SUGGESTIONS FOR DEVELOPING ACTION SKILLS

Based on these fundamentals, here are ten battle-tested suggestions for developing the action skills that get more done:

Spread decision making

With spread responsibility goes spread decision making. A business where too many decisions are made at the top is run by fear, because the CEO is afraid to trust middle managers to make decisions without his approval. He thinks this is the way to *control* the business and prevent things from getting out of hand. Whatever he may tell his board of directors about his tight control, he has, in reality, turned his executives into suggestion machines submitting everything for the boss's approval. This is really driving with the brakes on. The flow of initiative is replaced by a bureaucratic network overloaded with procedures and roadblocks.

The classic management principle is that decisions should be made at the lowest effective level. If, as part of your turnaround effort, your business can be transformed from restricted to broadly delegated decision making, it will release a burst of energy at all levels that should bring a dramatic improvement in results. It will certainly save an ocean of time up and down the line and help all concerned to be better managers.

Shared top decisions

On matters that properly require top management decision, the CEO, before exercising his responsibility as the final decision maker, should have the benefit of firm recommendations from his top management associates, as well as any specialists at lower levels whose opinions should carry weight. The solitary decision maker who has no need of supporting input may make a right decision because of his insight or genius, but he is building a ball team with only one hitter. Participative decision making at the top of an organization does not in any sense imply weakness or indecisiveness in the leader. On the contrary, it says that the boss, without compromising his chief responsibility, puts a high value on his people's independent thinking as well as their individual responsibilities. And the motor is running with all cylinders firing.

Bottom-line responsibility

Many businesses limit achievement by curtailing knowledge of and responsibility for profit to a few top management executives. This is a holdover from the era of the rolltop desk, when the boss kept all the "secrets" to himself and told his employees as little as possible. But if the team is to win the game it must know the full score. Top management needs many partners focusing on the ultimate score of the game, the net pretax profit. This not only releases more energy and drive in the members of the team, but it also trains middle managers for broader future responsibility. Many leading companies have moved from holding middle managers responsible only for their "contribution" to profit in the areas of their immediate responsibility to holding them responsible for their pretax net profit, even though it is affected by items not under their direct control. After all, the CEO himself does not control all the items on the operating statement, which include taxes, government-triggered expenses, and the effects of outside factors like legislation, strikes, and weather.

Managing time

The useful technique of keeping a detailed log for a few days can be of great help to the executive who is wrestling with the time problem. If he can look at an unretouched picture of exactly how he is spending his time he can go on from there to evaluate each activity's importance to his job performance and come up with remedial improvement. Armed with this information he can begin to plan intelligently the shape of his day. It takes will power and skill to adhere to a prearranged daily pattern, but this is an essential goal for maximizing executive productivity.

Memo barrage

A memo is a way of communicating information with precision and durability. But it is one-way and therefore not really communication until another memo is written in response. Thus memo writing tends to proliferate. When the boss writes a memo he may think he is saving time, being able to get rid of the matter then and there. But the subordinate must take great pains in fashioning his reply, because it becomes a matter of record, and this eats up a lot of time. The results-oriented boss, therefore, does better handling these matters at regular meetings with his subordinates, when he has the advantage of face-to-face reaction and can handle correctional items with much less damage to morale than by putting them in writing.

Meetings, the time glutton

If executives are asked about the sources of their time problem, the most frequently mentioned culprit is meetings. Meetings are a necessary and useful medium of communication and interaction, but they need to be managed so as to avoid squandering many people's time. Spur-of-the-moment meetings work havoc with everyone's plans and should be avoided. A meeting agenda and prepared material should be circulated well in advance, with the understanding that all will have read it before the meeting and come prepared to discuss the stated questions and reach decisions. The length of the meeting should also be announced on the agenda and adhered to by the chairman. With these precautions meetings can become an interesting and stimulating part of the job and actually save rather than squander time.

Telephone tyranny

It is not known by what stroke of genius Alexander Graham Bell endowed his instrument with an irresistible claim to immediate attention. Conversation with live persons present immediately stops in favor of the unknown caller behind the ring. The best remedy for telephonitis is the call-back procedure, administered by a secretary, which has by now become more or less accepted practice in well-run offices. Yet there are thousands of hours of highly paid executives' time wasted by sitting at their boss's desk while he talks on the telephone. He should use the call-back technique to save his subordinate's time as well as his own.

The workaholic

Devotion to the job and unstinting application to its responsibilities and objectives are admirable. But the workaholic who daily comes home late to a delayed dinner lugging a bulging briefcase that becomes two briefcases on weekends isn't necessarily getting more done. The monotonous grind dulls and stales the mind. What distinguishes superior performance from the average is often a creative idea or a flight of imagination, and for this the mind needs the stimulation of variety, awareness, and participation in what is going on in the world. In the end, an executive's total performance reflects the whole man that he is. He will not raise his level of achievement by opting for the life of a drudge.

Face-to-face communication

There is no better stimulus to action than the planned visit by the boss to the department or operation under his supervision. People prepare for these visits assiduously, and if they are handled in a constructive and participative way, they leave people excited about the management's interest in and support of what they are doing. The boss, for his part, learns more about his team when he sees them in action than in any other way. For similar reasons, it is a good idea for the boss to regularly visit his subordinates on their turf at headquarters. When the only place people see the boss is in his office many leadership and motivation opportunities are being lost. Leadership thrives on easy visibility.

The secretary as guardian

One of the main objectives of a good executive secretary is the management of her boss's time. She should read up on the subject, manage the telephone hour and call-backs during the rest of the day, foster punctuality, relieve stress by radiating calmness and good humor, and make visitors, especially subordinates, walk into an atmosphere of warmth, friendliness, and optimism. Any executive who has such a jewel is blessed, and the personnel department can make a tremendous contribution to executive productivity by developing a corps of this kind of executive secretary, supported by title step-ups (administrative assistant, assistant) and appropriate compensation for this very key function. Moreover, the wise executive keeps no business secrets from his secretary. The more she knows about what is in his mind, the more she can help him to function at his best.

PART VII

Monitoring Performance (The Pilot)

I had ambition not only to go farther than any man had ever been before, but as far as it was possible for a man to go.
—Captain James Cook

37

The Pacemaker Manager and Awareness

Get the facts, or the facts will get you.
—Thomas Fuller

THE REMAINING KEY FUNCTION

At this point things are pretty well in place for the turn-around. We have the Will, the Vehicle, the Road Map, the Motor, and the Fuel. More specifically, we have the necessary mind-set and determination, the underlying principles for success, the team, the planning, the strategies, and the motivation.

But what remains is very important. All this effort can come to naught if management fails in the key function of *monitoring performance*. Disaster is ready to pounce if we take our eye off the road ahead.

MANAGEMENT BY ASSUMPTION

How often, in the wake of tragedy, have we heard those sad words: "Well, I just assumed . . ." The architect assumes that the engineers know what they are doing, the head of the engineering firm adds his assumption that the draftsmen are following specifications precisely, the building inspectors, the owners, add their layers of assumptions. Later, when the roof falls in, the investigation tries to determine just who was at fault, and it is always difficult because of the complicated web of responsibilities and approvals.

EXPECT WHAT YOU INSPECT

At the heart of these serious malfunctions, which occur all too frequently, lies not a shortage of know-how or a lack of integrity but a breakdown of supervision. In our society today complex undertakings of all kinds require of those in charge a heightened awareness of what is happening at the key checkpoints throughout an enterprise. And this broad awareness involves monitoring performance *with insight* at all levels of a business, without hurting initiative, decision making, risk taking, or motivation. Monitoring performance has become one of the indispensable action skills.

So in a turnaround situation it is a good idea to develop a low tolerance for assumptions as a basis for action. Any businessman who has experienced that telephone call in the night announcing an unexpected disaster will have learned the bitter lesson of how dangerous it is to assume that anything is as it is supposed to be, without checking it. *Delegation* should never be *abdication*, and the manager dare not *expect* what he does not *inspect*.

THE PACEMAKER MANAGER

The pacemaker manager is one who *keeps the pace of achievement high* in those who report to him. To get the desired results through people, he has developed the knack of seeming to know everything that is going on, without slowing up his people or doing their thinking for them. These are some of the lessons he has learned:

The watched pot does *boil, sooner.* People do their best when they know that higher levels of management are in touch with what they are doing. They are turned off when the boss is never around or seems to know little about their problems and achievements.

People want partners, not takeovers. Especially those with most potential want to share the fortunes of battle with the boss, and are stimulated by the feeling of participating in total company endeavors.

People need encouragement and a pat on the back when things are going well. The *recognition* of success is one of the most powerful generators of redoubled effort.

People appreciate support and confidence when things are not going so well. The pacemaker manager realizes that discouragement can be paralyzing, and knows when someone needs to be bucked up.

SOURCES OF MANAGER AWARENESS

God gave us two eyes but ony one mouth, a hint that we should do more observing than talking. The people working for a good supervisor feel that he knows all about what is happening and is confident of their ability to get the desired results. Three main sources of input serve your awareness as a manager:

Personal observation

There is no substitute for the *feel* of a situation you can get through personal observation and contact, in the following ways:

1. *The regular one-on-one meeting* with your subordinate at a set time, usually weekly at the higher levels. The

subordinate does most of the talking, bringing you up
to date, airing problems, and commenting on developments in his action programs. You listen, offer suggestions, and bring up any matters he has saved for the
meeting.

2. *Touch-base sessions on objectives*, handled similarly.
Where difficulties are being encountered, these sessions
may be more frequent than when things are going
swimmingly.

3. *Breakfast or lunch for two*. When you sense that one of
your people is having unusual difficulty and needs
help, it may be most effective to suggest breakfast or
lunch together. The more relaxed mealtime atmosphere will be appreciated by the subordinate, who is
undoubtedly uptight about his problems and might not
be at his best in the boss's office. A variant of this technique is for you to suggest a meeting in the subordinate's office, with the latter sitting *in his chair* behind
his desk. These small sensitivities can be important in
getting people to open up so that you may gain below-
the-surface insights into the root causes of lagging performance. Quite often these have to do with personal
matters reluctantly talked about.

4. *Group meetings*. Well-managed companies have periodic meetings for a group of executives at the same organizational level at which top management and staff
executives present programs, place emphasis on priorities, and have members of the group make presenta-
tions of notable things they are doing, for the benefit of
the entire group. This kind of meeting in which all are
expected to participate in the discussion, is very helpful
to top supervision in learning more about the reasons
behind success or failure in the company. Moreover,
seeing each individual with his peer group helps to
identify strengths, weaknesses, and potential in the
group.

5. *Visits*. When you take a trip and visit one of your people on his own home ground, you are doing the maximum for your awareness. The stage is set for communi-

cation. The encounter lasts much longer than it would be at a meeting, there are several meals together, and perhaps a visit to the subordinate's home — all conducive to the candor that comes from getting to know each other better.

6. *Skip-level communication.* It is a mistake for a supervisor's communication to be *confined* to those who report to him. Try to have it understood in your team that a certain amount of informal contact below direct reporting levels is healthy, desirable, and does not involve either snooping or giving instructions from on high. Such contacts have a beneficial effect on the employees, who are flattered and stimulated by the apparent interest of higher management. They also provide valuable insight to the supervisor on the way things are going in different parts of the business, and occasionally things surface that would otherwise have been bottled up. In addition, the supervisor gains valuable firsthand impressions of people potential at levels below the one he directly supervises.

Customer feedback

In parts of the business where it would be appropriate, reliable input from customers can provide an authoritative outside opinion about company performance. As this relates to the people reporting to you, it is a useful and important means of monitoring performance. Sources of this input are complaints and other unsolicited comments from customers, as well as appropriate market research.

Management information systems

This all-important resource for monitoring performance offers great potential, but demands considerable expertise in a highly technical area to get the best possible results. This is dealt with in the next chapter.

38

Management Information Systems (MIS)

Each crisis you go into is on insufficient information.

—Robert Frost

THE AGE OF INFORMATION

The means of gathering and disseminating information have grown so explosively in our time that this has been called the age of information. Computer technology, an American product, has now reached the point where the kinds of information once dreamed about by managers are readily available.

But this very availability often leads to *informational overkill*, and the accordion-pleated pounds of printouts result in heavier briefcases instead of lightened tasks. Yet the state of the art in data processing, with viewing accessibility on screens instead of printouts, now promises a kind of informational millennium for those with the skills to adapt it to their needs, a world of fewer reports and far more data instantly available to management. The art of management has rarely had such a challenge and such an opportunity.

When we look at a turnaround company there is often a lack of the kind of management information needed to focus attention on results improvement. Or else the information is there but it has to be dug out of long and complicated reports that are not pointed toward action. And frequently there is not much urgency about getting reports out as soon as possible so as to stimulate prompt action.

MIS, A TOOL FOR RESULTS IMPROVEMENT

A turnaround company should look at MIS as a tool for improvement of results and not just as an adjunct of financial accounting. When management approaches MIS in this way it becomes one of its major action skills.

GUIDELINES FOR EFFECTIVE MIS

Here are some guidelines for *maximizing the return on the investment* put into management information systems:

1. Management's attitude to MIS should be *active*, not passive. It should look upon MIS as an aid to better and prompter decision making. Put more strongly, the *purpose of MIS is to* force *action*, not to maintain a reference library of interesting information. Because MIS is impersonal, it can do effectively and without offense the necessary job of reminding and needling the manager into taking action where it is needed.

2. To serve this purpose, information should be designed to *grab the attention of the executive* and direct it to the most action-suggestive data.

3. Through emphasis, *MIS should help the executive to remember important numbers*. High achievers generally know their key numbers by heart, the way they know their own telephone numbers or the names of their children. An executive who carries no operating figures in his head and must stop to look up everything is not *mentally on line* with his business and therefore not as involved and motivated as he should be.

4. In order to force the right kind of action, *MIS should stress plan and goal/objective*, not just last year.

5. *MIS should reduce labor content*. Spurred on by available technology as well as the example of the Japanese, American industry is moving into automation at an unprecedented pace. New attractive investment payoffs in various industries and a growing number of business functions are the motivating power behind this budding revolution. The turnaround company, because it may have been behind the parade in computer technology, now has a golden opportunity to move boldly and profitably into this new area of improvement. Of course, such a program needs to be carefully researched and supported by conservative projections. But the opportunity to reduce the labor content of the business and increase productivity should be pursued.

6. *Reliable and conservative accounting*. Nothing undermines achievement in a company faster than inaccurate or unclear accounting and financial information. MIS must set a high standard of quality and punctuality in reporting. Moreover, conservative accounting practices are the hallmark of good management. They lend quality to a company's profits and foster sound management thinking. It is a bad sign when a company starts to squeeze for better-looking profit statements by bending the sound rules of accounting practice.

7. *Competitive viewpoint*. Just as it does with so many other factors in the business, management should look at MIS competitively. If the competition is giving its people better information for decision making and prompt action than your people get, you are just as much at a disadvantage as if your products and prices were outdone. Periodic comparisons of this kind, backed up by professional analysis and cost-effectiveness projects, are recommended.

WHAT MIS SHOULD COVER

Following the above guidelines, MIS should use the best data processing techniques the company can afford on a payout basis to provide the ideal information for achieving the company's objectives. In most cases the following would be included:

Profit and cash flow components

The flow of profit components, from sales through gross profit and expense components to pretax net profit, plus the same on cash flow, are obviously *the key scoresheet* of your business.

Profit centers

In all but the smallest companies, executives are charged with the responsibility of running a segment of the business that can be considered a *profit center*. That responsibility needs to be recognized and helped by MIS with regular information on the flow of profit components for each profit center. As mentioned before, it is recommended that for the best results these reports should cover all the profit components down to pretax net.

Functional information

Moving in from the general profit picture, MIS should produce information showing performance on specific objectives, strategies, and special problems. In other words, MIS completes *the five-step professional management chain* from the conceptual to the actual, as follows:

Job description
Standards of performance

Objectives
Programs for achievement
MIS for monitoring performance

For example, product mix, inventory control, productivity, and expense control are all areas where a regular information flow should give the executive what he needs to monitor performance and react promptly to changing conditions.

Monthly forecasts

Professional management seeks to eliminate surprise. Therefore, where management is fully in touch with its business, the monthly operating report should rarely deviate much from what the management expects. Accordingly, MIS provides interim forecasts to give management early warning on what the results are shaping up to be. Thus, in the last week of the month, a forecast is made for the next month's results based on the latest operating trends. This gives management a last chance of doing something about what looks like a coming disappointment. In addition, MIS can provide a second forecast one week before the end of the month on how the current month will probably come out. This is probably too late for remedial action in the current month, but it is valuable early intelligence on changes in profit component trends that may be threatening performance in the next months. These tools work to make management look ahead rather than backward in its monitoring of performance, thus avoiding the prevalent evils of management by postmortem.

Financial reporting

The integrity of a company's financial statements and how they relate to the operating information used to manage the business are of the first importance. To support that reliability and integrity, *the internal audit function* has grown apace in recent years, along with an expanded role for audit committees on boards of directors. Slimmed-down staffs brought about by expense pressures and the inherent vulnerability of the computer to malpractice have increased a company's exposure to possible irregularities in financial accounting. Strong internal audit is the answer, and while the payoff is not always measurable, it is, nevertheless, real.

39

Shaping MIS
for Results

*Don't give the people what they want; give them
what they ought to want.*

—George Bernard Shaw

THE LANGUAGE OF INFORMATION

The language of MIS, the way it is put together and presented for use in management, can make or break its effectiveness as an action skill. A speaker may be the world's greatest authority in his field and have a tremendously important message to convey, but if he can't put his thoughts into a logical sequence and project them in a way that is understandable, forceful, and interesting, the message is *not received*.

In turnaround companies the information format has often grown up piecemeal, different parts of it reflecting what different executives along the way asked for. A collection of reports created on an *à la carte* basis necessarily lacks the overall coordination and guiding principles needed to sharpen MIS into a key management tool.

To help a turnaround it is not necessary to have the ultimate in automated information systems, but applying at least some of the following design suggestions will be helpful.

Fight overflow of information

Inundation with paper is one of the general complaints of American management. Part of it comes from the piecemeal addition of reports without eliminating others, and part of it can be blamed on the computer. "The computer is a moron," said Peter Drucker, because it will do whatever it is told to, ad nauseam. And once the programming is done, the printouts roll on and land in stacks on your desk. So one of the first steps in sharpening up information productivity is to eliminate unnecessary and redundant information. Try to elicit candor from your teammates as to what received information is not used. Another technique successfully used by some companies is periodically to omit sending out a report to find out if it was missed and by whom.

Combine related data into fewer reports

Piecemeal development of reports inevitably scatters the same information into various different reports. If the guiding principle is to *design reports that force action*, then the information relevant to your profit center should be presented in the proper sequence to help you see cause and effect in the results reported. Armed with that, you are ready to move to the next step, *informed action*.

Stress clarity of meaning

Wondering what an item means is a distraction when you read a report, and any distraction slows you down. The meaning of everything on the report should be self-evident and require no explanation. Caption abbreviations are good because they save space, but they should be spelled out in a box. The period covered by the report should stand out, and it is a good idea to have the date issued in the upper right hand corner of every MIS report.

Simplify numbers

If the report is aimed at action then there is no need for pennies, less than hundreds or thousands depending on the size of the company, more than one decimal in percentages, and so on. To help managers remember meaningful numbers, leave out the meaningless ones.

Percentages and ratios

When someone says, "My sales are $150,000 over plan for the month," it is obviously better than being behind plan, but there is no way of knowing how good the performance is until you relate it to the amount of the plan, as in "I am ten percent over plan sales this month." To help action, the report should anticipate your needs for decisions and save you work by feeding you the kind of relationships you need, in the form of percentages and ratios. It is amazing how many companies put out sales reports without percentages, expecting their people to make the necessary comparisons, or alas, just forget about it.

"Better or worse"

It is useful when a report gives the difference between actual performance and plan. But for maximum impact on action, label this "better or worse than plan," with the "worse" identified with a minus sign or parentheses. A label like "deviation from plan" is too neutral and mild. "Better or worse" packs an emotional impact and stimulates the adrenalin flow.

Timing

Reports should be issued at the earliest possible moment, because stale figures lose their potency. The frequency with which they are issued should be related to the pattern of action. It will be found that some reports will not inhibit action if they are issued quarterly, semiannually or even annually.

Size

It is a boon to the user to standardize reports at letter size (8½ x 11 inches) so they fit into briefcases. Where a larger report is needed, it can be folded into a letter-size format. Unwieldy reports are hard to use, depressing, off-putting.

Miniaturization

Reducing copying machines can transform your 8½ x 11 inch report to a quite readable 4 x 6 inch size. For upper-level executives who receive a good many reports, it is a real blessing to reproduce them in neat little pocket-size booklets that go anywhere. This is the ultimate escape from the paper deluge.

Coordination between division-produced reports and corporate reports

In a large organization with subsidiaries around the country, this step can be important. While the division management will want its autonomy, corporate standards for the design and content of MIS should be negotiated and followed. Moreover, new computer technology will offer attractive economies through centralization that should be hard to resist.

The screen

The new technology is lengthening the geographical range of computers by means of distant cathode ray tubes connected on line to central computers. This *on-line inquiry capability* represents a brave new world of management information, in which the executive sitting at his C.R.T. screen can ask the central computer for any information he needs. This will hardly solve turnaround problems just now, but in any given situation it is certainly worthwhile to check out the feasibility and cost effectiveness of such new techniques.

Bottom line

Although it has been mentioned before, any list of MIS suggestions should include the value and importance of computing and disseminating profit center pretax net profit figures, with proper emphasis, as widely as possible in the organization. The more bottom-line consciousness there is, the better.

Cost effectiveness

One should never forget that MIS is an investment, and like any other investment it should be justified by the return it produces. Especially because the data processing field is one of constant and rapid change, the whole management information setup should be looked at periodically for cost effectiveness, and updated where and when advisable.

40

The Flow-Through Concept Helps Profits

Fool me once, shame on you; fool me twice, shame on me.

—Chinese proverb

THE CORE OF THE PROFIT-BUILDING PROCESS

In a turnaround situation the entire management team is doing hundreds of things aimed at improving sales and profit growth. In that kind of environment it is tremendously helpful to pull that diffusion of effort together and focus it on the core of the profit-building process. To fill this need *the flow-through concept*, as presented in this chapter, was developed. Where used with the proper emphasis, it has proven very effective as a stimulator of results.

The more we live with the quest for the source of high company performance, the more the following becomes clear: If management does all the constructive and professional things covered in preceding chapters, if it has a good team working with well-developed plans and strategies, focused on objectives in a professional MBO environment—there is still something more needed. That something is the strong and constant *linkage* between what people say they will do and what they actually do achieve, between the plans and objectives and what comes out at the other end of the complicated corporate performance machine—the final result.

Flow-through provides that linkage simply and dramatically. As used here, the term means: *Of each dollar of increased sales, how much flows through to the bottom line. (The sales increment can be over plan, over objective/goal, or over last year.) The flow-through number is the percent of the increment that flows through to the bottom line.*

The manager starts out to get sales growth. When he achieves this, those dollars of additional sales have to run through a line of tackles that are out to stop them from getting to the profit goal. Markup margins, markdowns and clearance allowances, inventory shrinkage, take their toll up front. Then come all the expense demons, direct and indirect payroll, occupancy, advertising and sales promotion, corporate expense, and so on. It is the manager's task to keep his eye on all of these obstacles and bring as much as possible of his incremental sales dollars through to the bottom line.

What the flow-through concept does is to focus the manager's attention on how well he is doing this all-important job. It becomes *the yardstick of managerial excellence.*

FLOW-THROUGH EXAMPLES

To clarify how the flow-through concept works, here are some simple examples:

Plan sales	$1,000	Plan pretax profit	$100
Actual sales	1,100	Actual pretax profit	130
Increase	100	Increase	30
		Flow-through over plan	$\dfrac{30}{100} = 30\%$

Scenario: the plan was made, the programs for achieving it were in place, and the expectation was that if sales were just at the plan level of $1,000, pretax profit would be at the plan level of $100. Then things went well, and plan sales were exceeded by $100. Now, how much of that *windfall* of $100 should make its way down to net profit? Expenses should have been under control geared to the expected sales of $1,000, so that the only additional expenses justifiable are the direct costs of handling the extra $100 in sales plus whatever overhead is allocated on the basis of sales. Therefore, beginning with the normal gross profit on the incremental $100 of sales, it is logical to expect, if all things remain under control, that the lion's share of that gross profit will make it into net profit.

FLOW-THROUGH DISAPPOINTMENTS

A flow-through of 30 percent is usually pretty good. Much of the time, however, flow-through is disappointing and the increased volume results in little, if any, increased profit, for any of these reasons:

1. The *gross profit margin has deteriorated,* perhaps because prices were slashed in the hope of producing the additional volume.
2. A *costly advertising and sales promotion* program was used to produce the additional sales.
3. Management, knowing that business was good, *relaxed its control of expense,* and the profit potential of the additional sales was squandered.

Of course, management properly takes risks like cutting prices for a promotion or beefing up advertising to get a result. And nothing should be allowed to stop risk taking, which is the vitality of a business. But when the flow-through is not there it tells us that something went wrong in the way the business was managed.

What went wrong was the planning. The price, the promotion, the advertising program, were fine ideas. But they should have been thought through in advance and *put into the plan.* If that had been done the plan would have reflected a dip in the gross profit margin and more sales promotion expense, and if these were already in the plan pretax net they could not have prevented the additional sales from producing a good flow-through to net profit, perhaps in the neighborhood of the 30 percent example above.

THE POWER OF THE FLOW-THROUGH CONCEPT

If a management is indoctrinated at all executive levels in the flow-through concept, if the flow-through percentage is shown regularly on operating statements, put into objectives, and stressed in performance appraisals, it accomplishes at least three important things:

1. *It trains executives* to do a better and more thoughtful planning job, in order to stay out of the doghouse on flow-through.
2. As a result, *the plans that management works with are more reliable* and less liable to produce the disappointments that come from wishful planning.
3. The executive is trained to *become a better overall manager* of his profit components, thanks to better self-discipline and more realistic decision making.

NEGATIVE FLOW-THROUGH

When sales come in less than plan, the result can be a negative flow-through, as follows:

Plan sales	$1,000	Plan pretax profit	$100
Actual sales	950	Actual pretax profit	70
Decrease	(50)	Decrease	(30)
		Negative flow-through	$\dfrac{(30)}{(50)} = (60\%)$

Obviously, the challenge in this event is to *minimize the negative flow-through*. With proper awareness of the soft trend in sales during the period, management must look for ways to trim expense or bolster the gross profit margin, although the latter is rarely possible in a period of declining sales.

There is a lot of sense in the old maxim that when sales are up, hold to planned dollars of expense; when they are down, hold to planned percentage of expense. With expense control at its best, it follows that the negative flow-through on sales under plan should not exceed the gross profit margin percentage. Ideally this is true, but in practice if sales are under plan for any length of time it is exceedingly difficult to hold the line of expense.

Here again, by emphasizing flow-through as a key operating number, management trains its people to be more concerned and become more skillful in piloting the flow of profit factors down to the bottom line.

OTHER FLOW-THROUGH

Figuring the flow-through percentage in the same way, there are three other forms in which the flow-through concept can be applied:

Flow-through over objective/goal

It is best to begin by applying flow-through to the plan level as shown above. When, however, the company is operating with two-level planning, (the plan level and the objective/ goal level at 3 to 5 percent higher in sales) then flow-through can be shown over objective/goal. This works best for high achievers, where the objective level is generally surpassed in performance. Without this there will be too many negative flow-throughs and the value of the flow-through approach will be lost.

Flow-through over last year

This variant of the flow-through concept is a good, tough-minded device, but again works best with high performers. The high inflation we have been living with takes a big bite out of flow-through when compared with last year. But, nevertheless, it has some value, because the stockholders, after all, look at how the company is doing compared to last year. Where 25 to 30 percent is a good flow-through over plan, when compared to last year, norms will be considerably lower.

Flow-through of cash flow over plan

With the vital importance of cash flow these days, one could consider using a flow-through yardstick on cash flow worked similarly as the example above, substituting cash flow for pretax net.

TRACKING THE FLOW-THROUGH ELEMENTS

To support the flow-through figure for each profit center, it is helpful to summarize on the same monthly report what actually happened to the profit components on their way to the bottom line, thus:

In the first example, the sources of the increase in pretax net of $30 might be shown as:

Gross profit from improvement in gross profit margin *rate*	$10
Gross profit from increased sales (at plan margin rate)	15
Expense below plan	5
	30

This breakdown is helpful because it illuminates cause and effect. In addition to showing how many dollars of profit flowed directly from the increased sales, it shows the positive or negative effect on those dollars by fluctuations in the gross profit percentage as well as revealing the expense control protection given to those profit dollars.

41

The Role
of the
Chief Financial Officer (CFO)

I may have faults, but being wrong ain't one of them.

—Jimmy Hoffa

THE CFO AS BALANCE WHEEL

The classic pattern of a successful turnaround manager is one with the knack of galvanizing an organization into action, capturing share-of-market, and developing sound strategies and standards. But in a turnaround, no one, no matter how gifted, is self-sufficient. With all his talents, the CEO needs a balance wheel to be most effective, in the form of a chief financial officer who can perform the vital role of supplementing the CEO's strengths with other necessary qualities. This is an ancient tradition going back to the monarchs of old who needed a grand vizier, a Cardinal Richelieu, or a Bismarck to achieve their objectives.

ROLE OF THE CFO

The role of the chief financial officer (CFO), or the controller as he may be known in a smaller company, is many-sided and includes the following:

Watchdog of company profits

Above all, he must be the watchdog of the company's profits. Not only the CEO but the board of directors as well should look upon him as a kind of pathologist in the operating room. He does not perform the operation, but he is relied upon to produce the analysis on which the operation is based. The CFO must be fearless in his role of defender of the profit. If there is ever any semblance of unsoundness that threatens future earnings, he is duty bound to speak up to the CEO and, if necessary, to the board. And if the CEO intimidates him or muzzles him, he does so at his own peril.

Champion of realism

Figuratively speaking, he is the champion of realism in the councils of the business. Enthusiasm is often the father of overoptimism, and when that happens the CFO is expected to steer the thinking back to a solid footing. He is as willing as any to take risks, but only when they are supported by sound thinking.

Supplies early warning

He is expected to give the company early warning when he sees trouble ahead. As the figure-man par excellence he has the telescope that reveals the distant cloud on the horizon, and should have the analytical ability to size up its potential threat accurately for the management. Even with the best of control systems, for example, commitments are sometimes made that will produce top-heavy inventories down the road. The watchful CFO can diagnose the trouble early enough to head off or curtail the future problem.

Insures reliability of projections

Important decisions are made on the basis of projections of results to be expected if the decision is taken. The reliability of such projections is an important responsibility of the CFO, because when a projection is off course, the decision may be dangerous. And to build up a tradition of reliability in projections the CFO sees to it that the ultimate results are regularly compared with their original projections for all to see and learn from.

Oversees planning process

Overseeing the planning process for the whole company is one of his major responsibilities. He is the in-house top professional planner and the chief exponent of how to maximize results through professional planning.

Guides financial policy

He guides the company's financial policy, its financial strategies, and the extent, timing, and source of needed borrowing.

Oversees capital expenditures

Capital expenditures are also a major area of his leadership. He sets up the necessary criteria and procedures, and influences capital expenditure decisions.

Watchdog of cash flow

He is also the watchdog of cash flow and sets the standards and procedures for cash management throughout the company.

Supervises financial reporting

Financial reporting is, of course, under his supervision. He is the guardian of the *quality* of the company's earnings by fighting any tendency to report higher earnings through less than conservative accounting practices.

Monitors performance

As the leader inthe company's monitoring of performance, he is in charge of the content and design of management information systems, guided by the following:

1. *MIS is not an* a la carte *service*, meaning that executives should not expect to order a report and get it exactly the way they want it. Their input is essential in developing MIS but in order to come up with a professional system that will be a competitive advantage instead of a disjointed hodgepodge, uniformity of standards, principles, and procedures must be observed.
2. *MIS design* should reflect that its purpose is to stimulate, even *force*, results-getting action.
3. Since even the best of MIS is worthless if not used, there should be regular *monitoring of the use of reports*, their frequency, and their distribution, to show up weaknesses and suggest corrections.
4. *Fight the paper deluge.*
5. Keep abreast of the fast-changing state of the art in computers and data processing. Periodically *test cost effectiveness of new programs* and act accordingly.

PART VIII

After the Turnaround

A poem is never finished, only abandoned.

—Paul Valéry

42

Conclusions

You wrote, "It is impossible"; that is not French.
—Napoleon Bonaparte

You have finished our conducted tour through the fundamentals of a successful turnaround. The blueprint presented is based on long experience and will apply, in whole or in part, to most turnaround situations. You will, of course, have to adapt it to your own conditions, assigning your own emphasis to the component parts.

Here are some *concluding obsevations* to keep in mind:

OUTSIDE HELP

Turnarounds, as we have seen, are complicated, with many facets that require different kinds of skills. No one manager has all those skills, so it makes sense to get outside help when and where needed. If you are turning around a *lagging department* in a company that has other similar departments, don't hesitate to visit several of the more successful ones and come back with suggestions for solving your problems. Usually the other fellow, even if he is a competitor of sorts, is flattered by your approach and glad to get someone to listen to how good his department is.

Similarly, if you are running *a subsidiary of a large corporation*, get all the help you can from the other subsidiaries that are doing well. And if you are the CEO of the corporation, you must know CEOs of other companies that you admire and with whom a day or two spent would be stimulating and profitable.

In addition, more and more companies are recognizing the need for *outside specialists* and are using qualified consultants to reinforce areas where the in-house capability needs to be supplemented.

TEAM CONTINUITY

Once you have built your management team, give them a chance to hit their stride in their jobs. Frequently the best performers, when given tough new responsibilities, take a while to measure up to them and tune up their performance to their usual high standards. As the saying goes: No one is as good as he looks in the first year or as bad as he looks in the second.

Many turnarounds have been derailed by continuing management turbulence. Of course, if you are sure you have made a mistake, you have to remedy it. But there is tremendous power in the synergism of an executive team that has worked together for years. You will rarely find a consistently top-performing company with a revolving-door procession in the executive suites, and some of the best ones have been able to achieve an astonishing lack of turnover in their management team.

Learning how to keep dynamic achievers in your company is an art. Among other things it involves competitive compensation plus "golden handcuff" arrangements, which make it financially desirable for the executive to stay with the company: stock options, deferred compensation, and the like. But just as important is the rapport and spirit prevailing in the company that makes working there not only financially rewarding, but a stimulating and happy experience.

STAY HUNGRY

When a turnaround has been achieved, human nature often opens the door to the beginnings of complacency. Remember that a turnaround merely gets you out of the doghouse and admits you to the ranks of the good performers. And while the objective of a turnaround may have been achieved, the job of effective management is never finished. You must fight complacency and maintain a high level of motivation toward ever higher objectives, so that your company's performance will continue to rise toward the top of its industry. Recognize success for the turncoat that it is: The sought-after goal, once captured, can turn into your enemy and be your undoing.

LOOK AHEAD

Successful companies are sometimes lulled into the feeling that their strategies are well established, and therefore management drifts into spending its time on current operations with little real effort on the long-range outlook. As we have seen, this has become a shortcoming in a number of American industries threatened by foreign competition, which commits substantial capital resources to long-range strategies.

Instead, when you have succeeded in a turnaround it means that you are doing relatively well in current operations. The next challenge is to go after the long-term potential, with continuing strong emphasis on long-range planning.

RESEARCH AND DEVELOPMENT

Along with this goes more commitment to R&D to help discover new strategies for the future. The effective CEO is one who can achieve *consistent* growth for his company. He must live mentally in the future and probe what lies way out ahead in the various fields appropriate to his company. These long-range strategies often involve big risks, so they require matching depth of analysis and judgment. Also, a fine line must be drawn in research activities between freedom to explore way-out possibilities and inventing a cure for which there is no known disease.

PLAYING IT SAFE

Caution is a virtue in reasonable quantities but it can also become a vice. Don't let your successful turnaround leave you with the feeling that you have made it, and from now on had better play it safe. If fear is too much in your picture it can rob you of the accomplishment that comes from risk taking. The pioneer spirit that fearlessly launched this country as a great nation is still the same fuel that moves high-achieving companies.

The ignored turnaround described at the beginning of this book is costing our society far too much in individual, corporate, and national achievement. A turnaround in attitude from ignoring to attacking our problems/opportunities would help move our country toward a durable resurgence of the American economy and away from the danger of seeing this democracy sink into a kind of "mediocracy."

Index